The Angel, the Wit

A 21st Century Journey to Enlightenment

First published in the United Kingdom by Lulu.com
2008
© Janine Regan-Sinclair 2008
All rights reserved

ISBN: 978-0-9559745-0-2

It is currently the law that authors and publishers must publish a disclaimer regarding the advice given in books relating to complementary therapies. As a complementary practitioner I am not allowed to make any claims as to the effectiveness of exercises or treatments referred to in this book.

Therefore the information and exercises given are intended as a guide only. Neither the author nor publisher can accept any responsibility for any effects resulting from any exercise or treatment included in this book.

The information in this book is not a substitute for professional health care and readers are advised see a medical practitioner in the case of illness.

The Angel, the Witch & the Warrior

Contents

1. Introduction

Have you ever wondered what it's all about? Life I mean. Does the same thing seem to happen to you over and over again? Does bad luck or good luck follow you around? Are your relationships a recipe for disaster or do they run smoothly? When you stop and take a look you will begin to see a chain reaction of people, places, events, feelings, etc all being reflected in the magical illusion we call reality. Do you want to change your life for the better? If you do here is your chance. I suggest that you open your mind as you read on.

This book is for those of you who want to find out more about the bigger picture, spiritual growth and healing. It will teach you how to keep your personal energy clear as well as the energy in your home (The tie cutting and energy clearing technique described later in this book is the most important exercise I have ever learnt, I use it every day).

Some of the events I have written about are ones that I have experienced and learnt from, some are other people's experiences, but the lessons are there nevertheless. Life and its ups and downs get easier when you have looked at the bigger picture and understand the way it works.

It has taken me a few years of researching and working with complementary healing techniques, looking for some answers as to the meaning of life and the pursuit of happiness. I have discovered that self healing plays a big part of it. My goal is to help others find the inner peace and wellness that I now have and to raise global healing awareness. Because by healing ourselves, we will heal the planet.

I intend to share the information that has helped me become enlightened with all who care to take a look at themselves and make positive changes, healing mind and body. It is also for those of you who want to integrate and refine the soul through self purification working towards the ascension of the planet. I will explain this further in the chapters ahead.

I have written this book very quickly, it was self edited and self published. I have been procrastinating for at least four years since I first had the idea, but I lacked the motivation to put it all on paper until I was given a digital dictaphone last year which helped make it happen. I would like to point out that it is not meant to be a piece of literal genius. I do not even consider myself a writer really but I guess I am now as I have written this and I have started work on another book entitled "Saving the world from my bath tub" which is about a healer who goes out of body when she is in the bath and travels to other worlds and dimensions, deporting aliens from this planet and co-creating with Source and the Galactic Federation. Basically, she cleanses the planet and the local Universe of negative energies and Beings in the pursuit of global healing and creating the perfect world. One for the boys maybe, although I think both sexes will enjoy it and get the messages if they look for them. I also feel a third book is in there somewhere.

You may find that the information in this book jumps from one subject to another and does not flow as other books do, I apologise for that but my intention is to open your mind to lots of different aspects in order for you to investigate further the ones that interest you. I also fall into the Autistic Spectrum Disorder category of people and have slight attention deficit disorder therefore I do skip from one thing to another quickly as I cannot help it, so please bare that in mind as you read on. It is meant to be a taster session of information that may help you lead happier, healthier lives and if you wish to also become enlightened through self refinement and meditation. Every chapter has something interesting, it is packed with useful knowledge and guidance from how to meditate, tie cutting and space clearing, the chakra system and journeying, to removing the seed fear of enlightenment and activating your DNA changes.

Some of the words in this book may come across as spiritual, but please don't let that put you off, as a lot of it is common sense when you think about it. Whether you are spiritual or not, you may learn something from the chapters ahead that will hopefully inspire you to investigate further into whatever area you feel drawn to and change your life forever, just as I did together with many of my friends and family.

The answers are within you and all around you, if you decide to take a look, using whatever means you feel necessary. The most helpful way to find them to me so far is by practising meditation. All you need to know will become clear, but you need to do a bit of reading to help you get THERE and take time out to reflect on what you are learning.

I was born in Coventry, England and the youngest of five children to working class catholic parents. I have always had a fairly open mind considering I was brought up a Catholic, but I stopped going to church when I was a teenager and decided that I did not agree with the teachings of the church and I thought I would be okay if I was a good person and tried not to hurt anyone. I had been taught that God would forgive you if you were sorry for your sins and that was all I needed to know at the time. I was thirteen and happy to believe that, but something deep inside me believed there was more to life than the solid things you can see and touch, there had to be!

I know better now and my beliefs have not changed in regard to the church, but I do believe "As you sow, so shall you reap" even though I am not a religious person. That phrase "**As you sow, so shall you reap**" stayed firmly printed in my young mind, even though I was not fully sure what it meant as a child.

At 17 years old I found a job as a trainee draughtsperson in an architect's office and went to college to learn building studies. I stayed in the building industry for about 18 years until I was 36 years old and I could stand it no longer. This was when my father died and I was at an all time low. I was so unhappy stuck in a 17 year relationship I no longer wanted to be in and with a job I dreaded daily. I began to have panic attacks and that was the beginning of big changes in my life.

On my 37th birthday I went to see a solicitor and soon after this I took my son and a couple of suitcases and moved out of the family home. My sister very kindly let us move in with her, she had a large 3 bed semi detached house and we stayed there for a year. During that time I ended up in hospital for over two weeks as my digestive system and bladder just stopped functioning. Knowing what I do now, I believe that I could not stomach any more unhappiness or stress and my body was shutting down. It took me four months to get well and I had some healing from a friend during that time. It was soon after my recovery that I attended my first workshop and began my training as a practitioner.

Not long after becoming a master teacher I developed my own system and copyrighted it in 2005; it is called Crystal Ki Healing. It uses very high vibration light grids and involves meditative journey work. Since then I have never looked back and I moved out of Coventry in 2007. I have a lovely new man and my health has never been better. I work on a voluntary basis in the oncology department of a local hospital where I have spoken to groups of out patients about the benefits of complementary therapy. I also work and teach workshops in a holistic health care clinic in Leamington Spa, Warwickshire, England.

Enough about me, let's move on to the information I have gathered and would ask you to consider. The following chapters touch on theories and beliefs from many different sources including books, television documentaries, the internet and some very wise people I have had the privilege to know and talk to along my life's path, especially my parents and my many good friends.

I hope you enjoy reading it and it helps you on your journey.

The Angel, the Witch and the Warrior

This book is dedicated to my father, brother, sister and nephew who are no longer with us but have been guiding me in spirit and a special thank you to my friend Joseph who sat me down and made me get on with it…thanks guys x

2. Why the Angel, the Witch and the Warrior?

This title was chosen with reference to me, some of my previous lives and my present purpose as a warrior of light teaching global healing awareness. About five years ago I learned how to journey through the different realms of existence through meditation. During one journey very early on in my awakening I could see myself from three different perspectives all at once. In the first one I saw myself as a young woman being made to walk the plank on an old ship and looking down on to deep dark waters; I was to be drowned as a witch, forced along the plank, I fell to my death.

I could sense myself feeling at peace as I sank into the dark waters, I was also viewing this as an observer from above as a bird, and as a sea creature in the depths of the sea. The death I saw was in the fourteenth century and I knew in my heart back then that I had been a white witch who healed people using herbs and potions. However I was not a real witch if there is such a thing, I was a healer, and I was being murdered for my work, drowned at sea, terrifying and cruel beyond words. This was the beginning of being able to see with my minds third-eye, past, present and future events. Precognitive dreams and visions were to be common in my life.

Later, a journey took me underground to experience a shamanic healing, the death of a Shaman as they call it. I could see myself being pecked to death by a large flock of birds. This sounds traumatic but what happened next was a beautiful transformation, I could see this beautiful white angel rise from the dead body in triumph, a re birth, like the phoenix from the ashes, I had shed my old fear and transcended to a new level of consciousness, this angelic being was pure of heart and resides within me till this day; hence the angel in the title.

I have seen many of my lives, some good, and some bad. I have even been raped in a past life which is why I felt vulnerable in dresses in this life. I also saw myself leading a troop of men on horseback, into battle and that warrior spirit is with me to this day. I realise and understand that I can release the old parts of my personality and rest easy in my "I Am

Presence" my higher self having guided me home, the pain is gone and I feel clean and clear these days. I am still working on my ascension process but I have cleared much trauma from my body on many levels.

More recently my transformation was from a butterfly into a clear being of light, just like a diamond "Crystal Ki".

I have been a witch, an angel and a warrior, now "I Am".

3. Empaths

It is difficult to know where to start so I have chosen to talk about empaths first as I am one myself. Many empathic people are healers or therapists of some sort. Being empathic (clairsentient) means that they feel or sense other people's emotions where as telepathic people sense other people's thoughts. Being an empathic therapist can be very useful when working with clients but it can also be hard work if you do not know how to stop picking up on the energy of others. It is important to set specific intentions and to protect your energy field if you are an empath. You may need to learn how to clear your energy field and place a protective shield around you to stop you from absorbing other people's negative energy.

Being an empath myself I find it hard to be in certain places for too long with supermarkets being one of the worst. I remember one instance of being in a supermarket and being overwhelmed with a tight feeling in my chest and feeling panic. I knew it wasn't my emotions and when I turned into the next aisle there was a lady having an anxiety attack which I was feeling too. It was terrible. I had to get home quickly and clear myself using the energy clearing techniques explained later in this book. It is my intention to teach these techniques to as many people as possible especially other therapists as it is very adaptable, clearing negative energy from people, property and even the planet.

When I was younger I used to feel the energy around me and I could get very distressed at times and at thirteen I thought I was suffering from depression. I now know I was picking up on the sadness and grief that my mother was feeling after the loss of one of her siblings. She comes from a family of sixteen children and at the age of 84 she now only has one sister and one brother still alive, so all of those deaths must have been heartbreaking for her.

My mother was the only person I knew who would refer to people as souls and she would say things like "poor wee soul" when someone was ill or had died (she is Scottish hence use of the word "wee"). She is an amazing woman who worked hard all of her life and retired at 76 under duress, due to health reasons. I honour her for the love and strength she has given me. She is an Angel and so was my father, he died seven years ago and I still miss him so much.

My empathic feelings are useful to me when I am working as often I can sense how a client is feeling without having to ask them. When I do not want to pick up the energies or vibrations from other people I set the intention that I am a divine channel for divine energy only and that nothing will stick to me. I just think it and it is done, that way I have protected my energy. This involves my aura being Teflon coated therefore non-stick so to speak.

4. Complementary/Alternative Therapy

Due to the increase in the use of complementary and alternative therapies on the market these days, most of us have tried or know someone who has dabbled in some sort of natural remedy. Whilst most developing countries only have traditional folk remedies, some surveys have shown that 35% to 50% of people in the affluent west where modern medical health care is readily available are happy to use more traditional therapies and techniques dating back to ancient Egypt and beyond.

Because of the popularity of complementary medicines the medical profession have begun to take these therapies more seriously, even allowing them to be used in hospital alongside modern medical care. The more holistic approach is taken as a better way to achieve optimum health and well being all over the world these days. It is now recognised that health is directly affected not only by our physiological condition but social, psychological, environmental and even the spiritual aspects of our lives, all contribute to a happy and healthy individual.

At last we have doctors and nurses who understand this and are training in complementary therapies as well as their medical training. Physicians and medicines only treat the physical symptoms; the complementary therapies treat the mental, emotional and spiritual causes of the physical symptoms. **You need to eliminate the cause to stop the disease returning**.

A combination of medical and complementary seems to work well with most problems. Some conditions such as chronic fatigue cannot be cured with medical procedures, yet results can be achieved with complementary therapies. I once treated a lady who had been on sickness benefit for ten years because of chronic fatigue. I used Crystal Ki on her and she was better after only three treatments. I found a huge dark cloud in the mental layer of her aura, removed it and filled the gaps with light. I'm sure you have all heard the saying, "I feel like I have a dark cloud hanging over me". Well that is exactly what had caused her illness and it affected her thoughts making her feel depressed and mentally drained which in turn lowered her energy levels. How much money has been wasted on benefits when a hundred pounds or so could eliminate the problem?

Many people give their power away to modern medicine instead of eating healthily and having a more balanced approach regarding the mental, emotional and spiritual needs of our souls. A lot of drugs just suppress the symptoms driving them deeper into the physical system of the body. People are left with miasms and the illnesses reoccur. To find a permanent solution or cure we need to find the root cause of disease and remove that.

The concept of miasms in homeopathy describes miasms as underlying causes for many known diseases. If the symptoms are suppressed by medication, the root cause of the illness goes deeper into the body on both a physical and energetic level and can manifest as disease in the internal organs. Holistic therapies aim to remove the root cause of the illness and to rebalance the energy centres, meridians, etc. The emphasis is on being in touch with all aspects of the psyche and self care. Dealing with emotional issues and expressing the emotions wisely. For example, you could eat good quality food, exercise daily and lead a fairly balanced lifestyle but if you bottle up your emotions, they will store negative energy in one or more of your organs in the physical body causing blocks in the energetic flow of your essential life force which can lead to illness and disease. Some are fairly trivial but others can be serious and even life threatening. Holistic health care encourages people to have a good diet, exercise regularly and to release mental and emotional issues instead of suppressing them. It also promotes spiritual health awareness such as meditation or gentle martial arts.

As we evolve as a species, we need to feed our spirit as well by doing some form of meditation or connecting with nature, whatever works for you. All aspects of the psyche must be given adequate attention in order to maintain balance and optimum health within the whole body. Psychoneuroimmunology (mind/body medicine) is the field of science that now states that health of mind as well as body are essential as they are intimately related and one is affected by the other.

As the Mother Earth changes her vibration and we ascend to higher levels of consciousness, it is paramount to move forward and care for our minds and bodies in whatever ways is suited to our individual essence. We all react better to certain treatments than others and searching for the right one for you is important. So please do try two or three therapies if the first one does not work for you. I have tried many and my favourite is massage with the emphasis on acupressure points in the body. I feel like I am floating after a good massage. I have tried Bowen therapy, reflexology, kinesiology, Crystal Ki, acupuncture, homeopathy, flower formulas and chiropractic treatments. I recommend all of them, they all worked for me.

You may choose to check out the reputation of the practitioner by asking around the office or the hair dressing salon, anywhere you meet groups of people really or you can ask the universe to guide you to a competent practitioner. You will get help if you ask. Anything you hear or see three times is a message from the cosmos and is sent to guide you, so be alert.

I have heard sceptics say that natural therapies cause the placebo effect. This is true in some cases no doubt but very few compared to genuine results from the therapy itself. A placebo is an interactive drug or treatment that is used in trials. A sugar pill for example is given to the patient instead of the real drug. I remember watching a documentary where fake operations were carried out in order to induce a placebo effect. They cut the skin open to make it look like corrective surgery had taken place, but that was all, and in this instance the man still had a damaged knee. After the surgery the knee problem improved. Why? Because the patient did not know he had received a fake operation, he was given an anaesthetic which put him out for a while and when he woke he had a scar and that was enough to convince his mind that the body had been repaired. Due to the power of the mind over the body, the knee repaired itself.

In some cases placebos had a positive effect on 30% to 90% of the people in the trials. My point is that some results which come from complementary therapy may be the result of a placebo effect and that is great, as a positive result is the goal no matter how it is achieved but most results are not due to placebo effect. They are the result of the rebalancing of the energetic bodies.

5. Exercise can be healing

There are many ways to keep healthy and exercise is very popular, for example swimming helps you to feel supported by the divine, it is good for your chakras and you can set your intention so that the water will cleanse you on all levels before you swim thus enhancing the experience. Intentions are extremely powerful as I will explain later.

Walking in nature is exercise that is excellent for all ages and it helps to align the chakras and create the energetic flow. It helps with spiritual and physical integration and if you are walking outside in the park or in the woods it helps to remove energy blocks, it clears the lungs and any cobwebs. Walking barefoot allows adrenalin levels to drop and induces relaxation. It is also very grounding.

Body building helps us to gain strength for challenges that we may face along our path and is excellent for all chakras as a strong body evokes a strong mind.

The martial arts are all good forms of exercise and help balance all chakras especially the higher ones and are excellent for spiritual growth and discipline.

Any exercise would be beneficial to your mind body and soul and it is important that you exercise on a regular basis to keep yourself balanced in all areas.

6. Positive Emotions

Research has shown that positive people are healthier than negative pessimistic types. Emotions such as hope and joy are powerful and produce self healing when positive thinking interacts with diet and exercise.

It is a fact that emotional support is essential and relationships are a vital part of leading a happy, optimistic life blessed with good health. Isolated people have more health problems as it is difficult to have a rich emotional life when you are alone.

Having a sense of humour helps; people who laugh a lot tend to suffer less with dis-harmony related to stress, fatigue, tension and depression. Laughter eases tensions in the muscles and makes us breath deeply which is good for the circulation and releases endorphins into the system (laughter is the body's natural pain relieving opiates). Mirth is a great healer, so my advice is to start laughing and then laugh some more. Laughter dissipates negative energy. When you feel good, life is a breeze and being happy is achievable even when you are ill. You will get better quicker if you laugh a lot.

A positive person will see the glass as half full, the negative person will see it as half empty. Seeing the half full version will lead to better health and will create your whole experience in the 3D reality we live in. As I mention in a later chapter, your thoughts and especially your emotions create your reality or at least your perception of reality. If you are a negative, pessimistic person and are not suffering from depression, you could self help by changing your perspective, thinking more positively and taking control of your thoughts. Instead of seeing yourself as a failure, turn it around and see yourself as a success for having a go in the first place. If you have depression, you will need some help either complementary or medical. I see a dark cloud in the aura of clients who are depressed. This is easily removed in one treatment or even using distant healing.

Every problem has a solution and by stopping and breathing deeply when confronted with a problem, we allow divine input from a higher source to guide us towards the solution. We fall over in order to learn how to pick ourselves up. That's life, it is cyclical, full of peaks and troughs; we need to know and accept that and to go with the flow. All learning situations are positive, so don't beat yourself up when you make a mistake; give yourself a pat on the back for trying and dust yourself down and have another go.

Practices like meditation and yoga all help to focus your thoughts and calm the mind and body. Thoughts can be changed by learning to take control of your mind. Next time you start to think negative thoughts, stop yourself and consciously think of something you love or a happy memory. This way you are taking control. Your mind is the slave, you are the master. If you allow it to run wild, thinking rubbish, it will. Learning to control your thoughts will change your life as they lead to the emotional feelings which are the creational power behind your reality. Balancing mind and body leads to a peaceful emotional well being.

Balance is very important. You are unbalanced if you only give attention to the nice parts of yourself and if this is not addressed and you ignore the dark side of yourself then the energy will eventually explode like a time bomb, even if you appear to feel centred and grounded, you are probably heading for trouble.

These pent up emotions must escape eventually and when repressed emotions surface it can be a nasty sight. If you feel angry, release it, stamp your feet, shout out, cry, do whatever it takes to get it out because if you don't you may suffer as a result. All emotions are there for a reason, they need to be addressed and worked through not ignored or pushed aside.

I found the following exercises useful when I needed to release old emotional baggage.

First set the intention that the purpose of this exercise is to help release any old emotional energy that is not for your highest good. Then repeat the following four phrases over and over for at least five to ten minutes or even longer until it stirs your emotions and brings them to the surface.

I Love You
I'm Sorry
Please Forgive Me
Thank You

Repeating these simple but powerful words may bring to mind a person you are in conflict with or an incident that troubled you. At this point we can be moved to tears and the tears are the important part as that is the natural emotional release mechanism in the human body. We have tear ducts in order to cry and release stress. Crying is essential to releasing and letting go which are vital to the healing process.

The next exercise involves writing a letter to the person you are in conflict with or about the incident that has upset you.

Set aside some quiet time alone and write a letter pouring out all of your pent up emotions and thoughts onto the paper. This is actually releasing the energy from your system as soon as you start to write. Once you have finished, take the letter outside and burn it. This transmutes the energy and purifies it. It is important not to read the letter again once you have written it. It may take a few sessions before you are ready to let go and forgive but this method can work wonders.

I once wrote a letter that took me six hours of stopping and starting as I cried like a baby all of the way through. I felt exhausted but a couple of days later I felt so happy and clear, I just knew that I had forgiven the people involved and had let go of the issues I had written about.

The best thing about these exercises is that they are free and anyone can try them. They really work, I know through experience.

7. Heal thyself

It had been six years since the death of my father and only three months since the death of my brother, Christmas 2006. This was when I had the first recall on my Pap test (smear) in February 2007; they said I had pre-cancerous cells on my cervix. I sought deep within me and knew that this was caused by repressed emotional baggage, a few good emotional crying sessions I hoped would help to release it allowing me to feel at peace and actually I felt quite positive about the results. But I never really found it easy to cry and after I had been to Sri-lanka on a spiritual holiday, had met a new man, moved house and then experienced the tragic death of my brother's son, who was murdered – well lets just say that with all of this going on it meant that I forgot all about the smear test.

All of this in just sixth months, it was just too much, and two months after my nephew's death, I was recalled for more tests, the results of which returned with pre-cancerous cells present. This time however they wanted me to go to the hospital for a colposcopy – "no way are they going to be cutting in to me" I thought, and I refused the treatment. I told only two people, friends, who were both first class therapists, both medically and holistically trained who said that they would help me if I needed them, I had all the skills needed to fix this. I did have a couple of treatments from them, but I did not work on myself until I kept hearing the word cancer over and over. Alright I thought, I've got the message, I had tried to ignore it, but thought better of it and meditated on the issue by doing journey work and asked the four layers of my auric body and psyche as I felt they could help me with the answers. I had read somewhere that it was possible to communicate with various aspects of the self and it worked, I found answers. (This is a meditation technique explained later in the book)

My higher self told me that the pre-cancerous cells would turn to cancer if I did not take action and start to work on eliminating them straight away; my physical body told me to only eat organic food and to cut out sugars, dairy, meat and bread.

A therapist friend during a treatment said that it was due to repressed toxic emotions that had been sent from my internal organs and had collected in my cervix. So I knew what had caused it but I needed to talk to my emotional body and find each situation individually and work on releasing the emotional issues attached in order to heal it. Most of it was hurt, grief and anger, related to my ex-partner and my family. Each day for three weeks, I would meditate, find the issue and deal with it, talking it through with the higher self of the person involved, forgiving them, letting it go, and filling the voids with healing light.

As I let go I would also visualise the bad cells as blackberries on a bush, and see my angels take them away a few at a time, ensuring that I dealt with each issue that was stored there. My mental body told me I was thinking too much and needed to retreat into myself for a while to concentrate on my healing process. I did spend a lot of time in my own head, and reading spiritual books, and doing preparatory work. My spiritual body said to raise my vibration by chanting, listening to classical music, and to meditate for peace and harmony within. My higher self had told me not to worry, that my soul had chosen for me to experience this so I could heal myself and have more belief in my abilities as a healer, practitioner and teacher. I felt calm about the answers, and worked on myself with faith for those three weeks. Then one day my spirit guide Peter, told me I could stop. It was clear, all negative emotional cell memories had gone – I felt a real sense of achievement.

I later called the surgery to book for another examination and to make sure all was well, but I contracted a yeast infection and had to cancel my appointment. These infections were something I had experienced on and off since I was twenty years old. At the age of thirty one I had an operation where the surgeon removed a section of the skin from my perineum in the hope that this would solve the problem, it sadly didn't; in fact it just resulted in a nasty infection and made me ill for two weeks and the problem returned some months later.

I was now forty two and the same problem was back, time to deal with it again. I spoke to a homeopath at the clinic I worked in and she said it was miasm and gave me four opium pilules, these are homeopathic remedies, she advised me to take one that evening and said that I would know when to take the rest.

This was a deep rooted disease, and I needed to look within myself to see where the cause of it lay and with the help of my higher self I was advised to take one pilule every three days and to meditate to find what had caused this ongoing condition in the first place. It wasn't too long before I could see the cause - my first love, he broke off our relationship when I was twenty years old, and it broke my heart. This is what had been causing the problem, I promptly did a tie cutting meditation which healed the pain and soon afterwards the problem had gone. This shows us that causes of dis-ease are not always in the same place as the illness: my broken heart had caused the infection in my base chakra.

I was then able to go back to the surgery and have another smear test to check that no pre-cancerous cells were present and awaited the results which came back still showing a problem. This confused me for a short while and I spoke to a friend about it. We decided to meditate and find out why it had not changed the result and were told that I had the re-test only six weeks after the treatment and I should have allowed the body eight to ten weeks to regenerate the cells. I also needed to work on removing the physical cells as well as the cell memory.

I went to my local surgery for another test. It showed the same result which meant me having to have a colposcopy test anyway. I was then told that the results were a waste of time because you need to wait six months between tests and I had only waited three, the doctor should not have taken the tests so close together. I would have to wait for another six months before I could be retested. This book would be printed before that six months was up, so I am still waiting for the all clear but I am positive everything is back to normal.

I remembered hearing about a little boy who removed a tumour from his body using visualisation techniques. He sent a Pacman (like the one in computer games) into his body to eat the tumour a little piece at a time until it had gone. This seemed very logical to me and I decided to do the same only the creature that came to mind looked like a worm or a leech. I created it in my mind and set the intention that it was going to remove the bad cells from my physical body piece by piece over a twenty one day period. I had been told that people can be programmed or deprogrammed over a twenty one day period and this intention was important as it was conditioning the energy of the treatment. I worked on myself for the three weeks until I could see in my minds eye that the cells were gone. Then I visualised the leech leaving my body. This seemed to have cured the problem but I will still need to have the test in five months time to have another test. But from what I have been told, these tests are not conclusive anyway.

I would just like to mention a quick word about miasms, the concept of which in homeopathy is seen as underlying mental causes for many symptoms in the body. If illness and symptoms are suppressed by medication, the root cause can go deeper and can manifest as disease in the internal organs. Opium pilules can treat miasms, which form in the body. My deep rooted issues had caused very irritating yeast infections, once this was detected and the opium pilules administered, it was healed and released from the body for good. You can contact your local homeopath if you think you need opium pilules.

8. How I Became a Practitioner

It was not really until I the age of thirty five and having experienced repeated stomach problems and continual infections and digestive problems that I became more aware of complimentary therapies.

My friend was a healer who worked with energy and the chakras and I decided to go for a treatment after my father died, and was really impressed; I could not believe how much better I felt after an hour's treatment. It was not long after that a group of my friends and I decided to learn how to do it.

I was instantly hooked, there were a group of five of us and my energy seemed to flow differently; they all seemed to have hot hands when we were working, whereas I had cold hands, with cold energy flowing out of them. Needless to say my self-esteem went down and I knocked myself thinking why am I so different how come I have I got cold hands. It was later I realised I was channelling different energies to them, they were all working with the earth energies and I seemed to be working with a higher vibration, and that was the difference in the temperature I could feel. The Crystal Ki energy is cool and looks like clear diamonds with all of the colours of the rainbow in it.

So I studied to become a Master Teacher and I attained that level quite quickly, two to three years is recommended, but I am one of those people that when I find something I love doing, I tend to go full steam ahead and that is exactly what I have done ever since with my whole spiritual growth, learning different forms of complimentary therapy and raising my conscious awareness on a spiritual level, seeking the truth. Only I prefer to seek the divine truth which may differ to other people's version of truth, as they see their truth from their perspective only, depending on where they are in their journey. Their level of consciousness will effect their perception of the truth. There is only one DIVINE TRUTH!

Over the years I have come across many different people from Shaman to people who practice witch craft, they were all very interesting but not for me and not my energy at all. I did learn a lot about psychic protection and how to retrieve energy that had been taken from me. I learned that having your energy stolen or sleep paralysis can be a form of psychic attack. It took me over three years to find out that someone I trusted had been either sub consciously or consciously draining 50% of my energy, via an invisible psychic cord. We all have invisible psychic connections to one another, they are energetic ties and some are good and some are bad. The bad ones need to be cut as they can be used to control or drain us.

Cutting the bad ones is a speciality of mine, cutting cords, cutting ties, cutting negative connections with people, places and even material items. It is amazing how much energy you can loose this way and it is also amazing how many people are pullers, be it on your heartstrings, through need, or through guilt, all sorts of things, I needed to be free of these ties, to be able to just be, that is why I learned how to cut them all.

I know we are all one on a spiritual level, but in the third dimensional world, I craved solitude and it has done me the world of good spending time alone, slowly letting go of more and more people who were around me, even though they were good people, with good intentions, but fair to say some would have held me back if I had let them.

Unfortunately the person that was draining my energy was one of those. I honour her spirit for the things that she taught me. But within a short period of time there was nothing more to learn from her and I became very despondent and disillusioned, then I was fearful because I considered her very wise and knowledgeable and a guiding light. I looked up to her, I guess I put her on a pedestal really, but I was new to all this and until I was in my late thirties I wasn't very spiritually aware, although I always knew there was more than this solid world. But psychic protection, using your minds eye or balancing chakras and all of the things which are now part of my daily life, were at that time something I barely knew about and I only knew two people who were that way inclined.

Then when I woke up, that was it; it was like a light bulb was turned on in my head. I started to learn about meditation, healing and psychic protection. I realised that psychic attacks were mainly my own fault because I was having negative thoughts towards a particular person and that person psychically attacked me as a result.

In general psychic attacks are a result of our energy being returned to us but sometimes the shadow self of a person may be attacking you in order for you to learn discernment and help you to see through their persona. The wise thing to do is to cut ties if this is the case.

The shadow self or dark side of our psyche is also sometimes referred to as the enemy within. It is the part of us that was created as a result of the choices we made in our lives. Thomas Moore in The Care of the Soul states that "The person we choose to be automatically creates the dark double, the person we choose not to be."

The shadow self contains all of our repressed emotions and cravings, our ignored needs and short comings. If you were treated badly by someone and repressed your anger and rage, those emotions become part of the shadow self which over the years can become a destructive sub personality if not confronted and healed.

The choices could have been career related and you became a solicitor to please your parents when you really wanted to be an artist. The shadow contains both positive and negative and there maybe light in the shadow that can be salvaged through recognition and healing. The light within may prove to be a brilliant artist instead of a mediocre solicitor proving that we should follow our hearts desires.

The shadow self will behave badly until it is given a voice and taken notice of. Usually the shadow demands attention as we hit mid life and this is when many people change their career and relationships, etc. It is now more important than ever to heal this shadow self in order for us to ascend to higher levels of consciousness.

Most people see the shadow as negative and try to ignore it only knowing themselves as persona and that is all that they allow other people to see. The persona is the ego aspect that is presented to the world for approval. It is a kind of mask and is not always a true interpretation of them. A person who spends most of their time wearing this mask is out of balance and blocks not only communication in relationships, but personal and spiritual development by ignoring the shadow.

The seeds for a happy future quite often lay within this rejected, repressed shadow self. On a psychic level, our darker side can actually cause people harm and needs to be kept under control. Your darker self can be manipulated by outside influence and it can actually psychically attack people either with or without your knowledge. It can also damage you and this aspect is referred to as the self saboteur. The problem is that you are responsible for your shadow self and if it is attacking someone, you are the one who receives the karmic consequences as a result.

The best way forward is to heal all aspects of this shadow and in doing so your life should change for the better. There maybe a repressed male or female side of your personality in the shadow and as human beings are psychologically androgynous, it is important to tend to these parts of the psyche.

In the past these aspects were brought to our attention as we hit mid life but because of the planetary changes taking place, age is no longer an issue and we can feel the need to seek healing and balance much sooner. Instigating these changes can be a form of re-birth into a completely new way of being. It is also important to attend to our spiritual needs through some form of meditation, yoga or similar.

The inner child is also an important part of the human psyche that needs to be cared for and healed. The inner child resides within all adults as the part of us that loves to play and have fun. A child who was abused or ignored and not correctly nurtured may have inner child issues in later life that form parts of the shadow self.

Healing this inner child can be very emotional for the person concerned but it is well worth the effort as wholeness and peace can be achieved. It is human nature to be nurtured and to nurture, loving and praising a child can sculpt them into wonderful balanced adults and parents.

It is important to tend to all aspects of the self in order to be a well balanced happy person. My inner child loves to walk along the beach with her feet in the sea collecting shells and if she's lucky she finds something special like a starfish. She found three on her last holiday, which was quite significant at the time.

9. Sri Lanka

I had been getting a strong feeling that I needed to go to India or somewhere in Asia for some time since Christmas 2006. I spoke to my friend but she could not get away until the summer due to her finals of a masters degree she was taking. It was early April and I just decided I was going somewhere; anywhere spiritual would have been okay with me. I asked my Angels to help me find the right place and within hours I was paying for a two week holiday in Sri Lanka and I was going alone.

A couple of weeks later I was on my way, I had only travelled a few times alone before, but this was the furthest I had been and I decided that it would be a spiritual adventure. The one thing that I specified to the Universe was that I wanted to meet a Buddhist Master.

When I arrived at my hotel, which at first glance pleased me, I was rather jet lagged and went straight to bed. The heat took time to get used to, as it was so humid. After a day or so I was acclimatised and reenergised.

The hotel was on a beach, the south west coast and I was inspired to connect with the sea and go snorkelling. I quickly found a guide and was off on the roughest train ride I had ever had, to a village on the south coast about an hour away from where I was staying.

I found the train journey a great culture shock compared to the trains in England, but fun nevertheless. My Sri Lankan guide was called Serj. He introduced me to his friends, one of which was a young Australian woman who had fallen in love with a Sri Lankan man and had been living with him for almost eighteen months. She was a lovely girl and I felt very comfortable with her even though I was old enough to be her mother.

We ended up snorkelling together and the water was perfect, with amazing coral and beautiful puffer fish and electric blue fish I had only ever seen on the television. We were in the water for about two hours before it started to get a bit too choppy.

Being a Piscean I felt really at home and the couple of hours we spent in the sea snorkelling, soon went by. After we had some lunch, Serj took me to see where his family lived. The house had three bedrooms and was around five meters away from the main railway line. The bathroom was a concrete room with a hole in the floor, a cod tap with a hose pipe attached with only a bucket to wash with. It was not quite a tin hut, but basic living would be an understatement. I realised that they were on low wages, but compared to living standards back in England, this was poverty.

Serj told me that he was paid around £40 a month for a nine hour, six day week. I earned more than that for one hours work at the clinic back home. The whole experience was a real eye opener. I asked him to take me back to the hotel and I gave him a £5 tip for being my guide for the day.

There were armed guards at the hotel gates, as had all of the hotels; it made you feel safe and uneasy at the same time. Can you imagine armed guards at the entrance to every hotel in England? No way! It made me realise how lucky I was to have the level of freedom I do back home.

The next day I decided to sit out by the pool and read my book. It was yet another beautiful day and I had already been for a dip in the pool to cool down. I befriended a couple from England and they said that they had been told about a beautiful waterfall where you can go swimming in cold water unlike the warm water in the pool. They were going later that afternoon and invited me along. I said yes, of course, the cold water was calling me.

We later met up with their guide Kalum, and went off in his tuk tuk, a three wheeled vehicle crossed between a bike and a car sometimes called a cabin cycle and very popular in Asia. The seats are not very soft for long journeys, the roads were full of pot holes and the other drivers were a nightmare, not to mention the odd cow and chicken roaming around in the middle of the road; it was certainly an experience in itself.

When we arrived, we had to walk for ten to fifteen minutes to reach the waterfall through the woods. When we arrived, it was the most amazing oasis, just perfect. We had to cross to the other side of the stream over the stepping stones. I had come prepared wearing my swim suit under my clothes; I took my trousers and shoes off and made my way to the other side of the stream. On the other side was a wall of stone and rocks about three or four metres high. Just beyond that was a beautiful waterfall about two metres wide and five metres high flowing into a pool about fifteen metres in diameter. The rocks had formed a shelf around the outside of one half of the pool just below the water level. When you were tired, you could sit on the shelf in the water and rest. Kalum climbed to the top of the higher rocks; there you could look down into the crystal clear cold water of the pool below the water fall. He dived in from the high rocks but I was not quite brave enough to try that. The water was fantastic, it was so cold just as promised, just what we needed to cool down. We swam for an hour or so in the cool refreshing waters of the pool and then we made our way back to the house. The house belonged to a friend of Kalum and having worked up an appetite we had some local cuisine before making our way back to the hotel.

I had decided that I was going to work on raising my vibration by cleansing my chakras and having plenty of massages while I as there. I meditated every day and in no time at all I could clearly see the Ascended Masters, Buddha, Jesus Christ, Lady Nada and Quan Yin, almost as soon as I closed my eyes, it was amazing. I was so peaceful and felt on top of the world.

Most days I would carry out some sort of cleansing on the land using light grids to clear Tsunami damage and sadness with the help of these Ascended Masters. I now realised why I was here and not in India. There was so much sadness in the ground and the atmosphere around Sri Lanka, it really needed cleansing.

The next trip I took was to a local turtle sanctuary. The locals collected the turtle eggs in a bid to keep them safe and protected. They kept them in tanks until they matured and could be released into the sea.

Some of the turtles were amazing, one of which was an albino who liked very much to be tickled. I was lucky enough to hold her, she was beautiful and so friendly, and I felt really honoured to have held her as albino turtles were rare. I was invited to come back later that evening and help release the turtles back into the sea, but I was unable to make it, fond memories of that amazing little albino turtle I tickled still remain.

During my time in Sri Lanka the locals were celebrating the birthday of Buddha, by bringing flowers to the temples and worshipping through prayer and meditation. The hotel manager had arranged transport to the local temple one afternoon and I decided to go along. It had a statue of Buddha that was twenty five meters high, and this impressive awesome site could be seen from miles away

However it was an experience before going to the temple I recall most strongly. As I earlier mentioned on booking this trip I had asked the Universe to ensure that during my trip I met a Buddhist Master, well it was on this particular morning that this actually occurred. The monk in question had come to the hotel to give a one hour talk about life and peace. I was most excited and had woken up extra early in the morning, bathed and dressed in white; I made my way to the conference room and was happy that I had managed to secure a front row seat.

By sitting at the front I was actually sitting within his aura which was amazing aquamarine with patches of yellow, the Christ/Buddha consciousness colours, and I could certainly feel it, it was blissful. The room was so peaceful, you could have heard a pin drop when this wise soul opened his mouth to speak to us, I could have cried, I felt so humbled by his tone.

He chatted about peace and that Buddhists do not speak of God but only of the Mind. This was fine with me, as I had known for some time that WE ARE GOD, God is the collective consciousness of all of us, one mind so to speak. However I felt his words may have shocked some of the people in the room.

The one point he stressed was that women should not feel the need to wear make up because we were beautiful enough without it. How right he was but the pressure placed on woman by modern society to look glamorous these days is so high. This meeting however was one of the highlights of my trip, and I have never seen those colours around another human being to this day.

It was later that afternoon that we visited the temple and before we left the hotel the manager came and gave me a bag full of white flowers. The flowers were an offering to be placed on each of the different alters at the temple.

It was only a short drive to the temple and when we I arrived I washed the flowers in cold water which was traditional and moved from one room to the next placing the flowers as I had been directed, on the alter in front of each of the Buddha statues and then saying a brief prayer. The temple was huge and had lots of smaller holy buildings around the main arena. There must have been 10,000 people; all walking bare foot from room to room washing the flowers they had brought with them to leave on the various alters. I was the only white person there and I felt like Hayley Mills in one of those old movies I would watch as a child with my father on a Sunday afternoon.

By the end of the day I was floating, having soaked up some of the monk's energy and praying and meditating all afternoon, it couldn't get any better than this. I felt nothing but total inner peace.

The whole trip was pulling me more and more towards the Buddhist lifestyle. Their wonderful altruistic philosophy seemed to be the way to live. You could feel the peace when you were talking to a true Buddhist, they emanate calm. Not being religious and against being labelled, I decided against becoming a Buddhist and to stick with my own union with Source, to just try and be the best person I can be and to be free.

I had a new spiritual guide come to me on that trip, his name was Matthew, and that was all I knew of him until one evening when another light worker, a beautiful woman in her thirties who was also clairvoyant told me she could see him. She said he was very important looking, wearing a long white robe and that he was blowing me kisses, saying that he loved me. I had another guide called Jupiter, a dolphin, a cheeky one at that, always smiling like he had not a care in the world. Whenever I had to solve a problem, he was there to help. Jupiter asked me to place my hand on the back of her heart and pass some information on to her. I asked her if that was okay and she said it was fine. I placed my hand on her back and she said that all that she could feel was unconditional love flowing thorough her heart. She could see the dolphin smiling and the connection was made. I felt she would see him again. Dolphins are amongst the wisest creatures on the planet and can teach us many things to help us raise our frequency and help heal ourselves.

Another highlight of my holiday was a visit to the elephant orphanage and my trip to the Temple of Tooth in Kandy, four hours north of Beruwela. It felt a lot longer than four hours on those bumpy roads I can tell you. The guide Kalum had hired a mini bus to take three of us on a two day trip.

The temple was amazing; it was like a large white and gold palace. The outside walls were covered completely in tubes of light and it was so bright you could see it for miles. The inside was just as beautiful, with carved statues and gold everywhere. There was a large golden cask that was said to house the tooth of Buddha himself but the queue to get near to it was horrendous and we were short of time. I did get a glance, it was all very impressive and a wonderful trip, I would recommend it.

I was allowed to bathe a full grown female elephant, a fantastic experience. I can see why people want to work with these animals full time; they are so loving and powerful. I was lucky enough to be able to get in the river with her and scrubbed her with a piece of coconut shell, she absolutely loved it, I could have stayed there all day. Afterwards I sat on her back and she got up and took me for a walk around the woodland. I was also able to feed her and tickle her tongue. For a short while I really felt connected to her and it almost felt as if we could read each others minds. I have heard about people who use telepathy to communicate with animals and for a while thought I could do it too. I placed my hand on her forehead and the words "I love you" came into my head. Was it her or me, I don't know. Something happened though and on a much higher level of consciousness. Maybe our higher selves were communicating and we could feel the vibrations. That was a heart felt moment, a universal gift.

I was so happy that day. These animals are so gentle and yet their power is phenomenal. I came back home a more content human being filled with peace and gratitude for the blessings in my life.

This trip was a turning point in my life and self development, in that I moved on very quickly when I returned home. I bought a property the week after I came home and met a new man as well. While I was away, I had made some notes for a book I was thinking of writing (this book) and I decided that I needed to stop procrastinating and signed up for a book writing course when I moved house.

That was just over a year ago in April 2007, I have come a long way since then and achieved more than I thought I could, I've written this book and I feel a bliss surrounding me that I can almost taste, it is so sweet.

10. Karma

In order to understand your life and how it works, you really need to know a little about karma. We create karma with every thought, word and deed, all actions have a reaction and they all have consequences to you, your family, people you interact with and your whole community, the whole world and no one can escape it. Karma teaches us how to behave, what goes around comes around. In general, if you're good to people, people will be good to you. If they are not, maybe you are being tested.

Karma helps us to evolve spiritually into higher aspects of being connected with the higher self, allowing us to be more compassionate, sensitive and wise. The thing you need to watch out for is the ego. The ego self is corrupt, this ego does not stop functioning when we are growing, and you can still find yourself relating to others from a selfish point of view. The ego needs to be conquered in order for us to progress.

What is karma? (There are basically four types).

The first is the result of all past life actions, your total cosmic debt. This is added to or reduced by your actions on a daily basis.

The second is the part of your past life karmic debt that has been worked on in this life. If you lessen your karmic debt in this life you get to work on more of your past life debts and clear them or not, whatever the case may be.

The third is karma that is added to your past life karmic debt based on your actions in this life. If you do not reduce your past life karmic debt and add more debts to this, they will be sent to your future lives to be worked upon.

The fourth is instant karma. It's created daily and is worked off immediately. It doesn't get added to past life karmic debt. For example, if you murder someone, you get sent to jail – debt paid!

Karma means "As you sow, so shall you reap" this means that you get what you give and it applies to all areas of life, it is about cause and effect action and reaction, justice will be done. Your karma is your responsibility and there is no escaping it.

Next time something bad happens to you stop and think, what did I do to bring this on, the answer will soon come. Remember thoughts, words and deeds create karma; badmouthing someone or thinking nasty thoughts about them are actually a form of psychic attack. It will come back on you; guaranteed!

Somebody cuts you up in your car and you swear and curse, stop and think! You're psychically attacking that person, creating bad karma for yourself. The wise thing to do would be to see it as a test. Just take a deep breath and let it go - test passed! If you are really wise, you might think, "Bless them, they must be in a hurry". When you bless someone, you are sending out very positive vibes and thus invoking positive karma for yourself upon its return, Simple!

Life is a constant cycle of birth, death and reincarnation. It exists in order for us to learn, Earth is a beautiful mystery school containing the secrets of success. The answer is simple and love is the key. We keep incarnating until we have learnt our lessons. It is all about spiritual growth and purification and Karma exists solely in order for us to learn, it is not about punishment, although it can feel that way at times; your crap is exactly that, your crap, you created it. Try to remember that! We are all in the same boat.

Before we incarnate (are born into this life time). We all agree to face certain trials and tribulations. These are the result of actions in our past lives, our cosmic debt. When we are born we have our past life memories erased. There are two reasons for this; one is to make sure we have really learnt our lessons in the past and the other is to stop us from being overwhelmed by all of that memory from all of those lives. Imagine all of that information in your head; it does not bear thinking about. The whole process is about evolving into higher levels of perfection, purifying every thought, word and deed. This applies to everybody whether you are spiritual or not. There are no exceptions. It is universal justice for all; it is completely fair and accurate. There are no karmic mistakes. For example: there are no innocent people in prison. They might be innocent of the crime they are incarcerated for in this life but they must have committed a crime in a past life and got away with it. Or, so they thought. There is no such thing as getting away with it, in this life, past lives or future lives. It all eventually catches up with you.

Karma will continue until we all become spiritual masters. It begins and ends with love, unconditional love. If all you give out is love, all you receive will be love, the perfect life. We are all on a journey through the school of life until we master it. We are here to learn and gain wisdom. If you choose love, tolerance, forgiveness and compassion; the lessons will be easier to learn, life will be a dream, problem free and a pleasure to be a part of. The choice is yours. We all get caught up in the karma of other people at some point in our lives and we can worry and get involved, and this is the worst thing we can do. The best thing to do is ask God to send them blessings and ask the angels to help them sort themselves out. We can help other people but only if they ask for it. Giving it away is interfering and not the wisest thing to do and can have repercussions.

We are moving into a new way of being and soon Karma will be a thing of the past as we ascend to greater levels of consciousness.

11. Science and Karma

History contains many theories relating to science. Sir Isaac Newton was at the forefront of documented scientific facts and figures when he published his Laws of Motion in the 17th Century. His modern (at the time) views explained that the universe is a huge mechanical system and that space and time are absolute within that system. In later years, towards the latter part of the 19th Century, information came about to suggest that other forces also existed. They could not be explained by Newtonian physics and were referred to as Field Theory. Research made by James Clerk Maxwell and Michael Faraday led to the discovery of fields of energy. They also stated that these fields closely interacted with one another.

By 1900 Quantum Physics was a part of the new world theories when Max Planck put forward his theory of the world as a burst of "Quanta". This showed that matter consisted of a burst of various possibilities and probabilities rather than being absolute as Newton believed. This developed into a whole new way of looking at things and it suggests that reality as we perceive it may not be so real or solid at all. Around the same time Quantum Theory evolved. This was a theory based on relative physics. It was Albert Einstein's view of the Universe which contradicted Newton by stating that the universe was relative rather than absolute (meaning it was always changing) He suggested that time and space were inseparable and coexisted as a fourth dimension.

Approximately 17 years later towards the end of the 20th Century, String Theory and M Theory were published. This proved that every single thing we can see in our reality consists when broken down into its smallest particles of strings of energy or light all vibrating at different frequencies. This helped to connect all of the previous scientific theories and in 1984 was formally accepted as the mainstream.

Maybe one day a single theory will be discovered that unites all of the other theories relating to the holographic nature of our world and beyond, the reality we see with our human eyes and the realms we see with out minds eye. The one thing we do know is that we create the hologram.

What connects Science and Karma? Well, if every action has a reaction, it must be either a positive reaction or a negative reaction, there can not be no reaction at all, therefore we are all creators. I was taught that we all have God within us and never really understood it, but if God is the creator and we can create using thought, speech and by what we do, we must have the power of creation within us, the ability to manifest certain things in our lives, not on the same level regarding the power of God, the creator of all that is, but the power to create never the less. This being the case, we must create our own lives to some degree if not completely.

By the word God, I mean the First Source & Centre, the First Creator, Grace, the Universal Master, the Great Oneness, whatever you choose to call it. I have chosen to use the word God (the First Creator) or Source as a term of reference. It is open to your own interpretation. I some times use the word Universe, so please bear with me on that one.

I once worked with a man who was very unforgiving of other peoples short comings and bad mouthed them constantly for silly mistakes they had made booking in his clients. One night, he had all four of his tyres slashed; he moaned and groaned about it for days. What he did not realise was that he was only producing more negativity and the cycle continued. His clients would either cancel appointments or turn up late. This did not happen to the other people with their clients. They did not moan about things that went wrong, they were much more laid back. Maybe if he had been more tolerant and less volatile, producing more positive energy, this may not have happened, maybe he would have only had one tyre slashed, this would still be annoying but most of us have had some form of negativity hit us at one point or another due to our ignorance or innocence of how life works. Nobody is perfect!

From my experience, I believe that the best way to break the cycle is to treat the trying times as a test; we are all at the school of life after all. We are here to learn whether we like it or not. If you choose to treat problems in life as a test, let's say you get a flat tyre for example; you can either fail by getting angry which just produces more negativity to come back on you in the future or you can take a deep breath and deal with it calmly and think 'Oh well, these things happen' and learn the lesson. Do that and you have passed; it is easy when you know how. After all, you must have deserved the flat tyre that is the way life works. The Universe sends it right back at you. So, just let it go, get it fixed and concentrate on positive thoughts, words and actions. Simple! By the way, a flat tyre does actually mean something, everything means something. A flat tyre could be sent to slow you down, it could be the result of negative Karma or it could mean that you are feeling flat or deflated either emotionally or physically. If it happens to you, just ask your higher self the question, "What is this trying to teach me?" And the first thing that comes into your mind is the answer.

When you act with Grace you create more positive energy for the future. Remember the saying, 'What goes around comes around'? It really does! When you stop and think you will start to realise, all things happen for a reason. On the other hand, when you are kind, considerate and forgiving most if not all of the energy that you produce is positive which means a brighter future. You will begin to notice the good things that happen to you along your journey like getting the bargain you have been looking for when you are shopping or a parking space just where you need it instead of miles away: the little things count too! You may even get the fantastic job you were looking for and the great salary. Basically, you get what you deserve, albeit good or bad. Accept it and move on. If things are bad in your life change how you live, fix it, if you need help, ask for it, ask the Universe. If you don't ask, you don't get! You create your own life, remember that! You are wasting your time and energy moaning or over analysing, it can send you around the bend! Enjoy the good things and give thanks and treat every day like it is your first and last; live for today, in the moment, that is all there is, this moment, right now. The past is gone, it no longer exists and the future has not happened yet, it does not exist, not in this dimension, anyway. There is only now!

If you find it hard to let go or relax, find some help. There are a multitude of ways to do it, for example; meditation or relaxation tapes or CD's are worth a try, If that does not help, you could try a complementary or alterative treatment, the choices are vast but the advice is not to ignore your body's tell tale signs, find the cause of the problem and get some help. If you ignore it, it will only get worse and damage your future happiness and your health.

Having met many different people over the years, I have noticed that the ones who were happy, cheerful and laid back had better lives on all levels. They were successful and the right kind of people came into their lives to help them on their journey. Like attracts like. Generally they were healthier and they were a pleasure to be around, their light shone so to speak. The ones that had a dream to fulfil and were positive and worked hard to get there usually did. On the other hand, the people who were aggressive, complained a lot or treated other people badly were not much fun to be around at all; in fact I avoided them like the plague. They seemed to have a lot of what they called bad luck; things just did not seem to go their way. If only they could see that they were creating their own bad luck, they might have changed their ways. Karma was intervening once again, you can not escape it!

However, I need to express here that not everything that happens to you is a result of your actions in this life. Some events have been predetermined prior to your incarnation (before you were born). They are for your own development. Lessons you have not learned yet and things you need to experience in order to grow as a person. Believe it or not, you actually agreed in spirit to certain things happening to you in this life before you were born. The notes about Karma explain this further.

I have explained as simply as I can the Science and Karma relating to this life, the infinite cycle of evolution and the journey to enlightenment. It is up to you whether you choose to believe it or not but it does make a lot of sense even if it is a bit mind blowing.

The questions is: Are we in a cycle of events in a matrix governed by mathematics and geometry or are we on a spiritual journey to reach enlightenment and all that we see around us is just an illusion in which to learn our lessons, a great big holographic school, if you like? Both make perfect sense having looked into them in depth, the connection is there; the scientific theory and the spiritual theory that explains creation and the meaning of life but you should try to reach your own conclusions. I have written this to inspire you to find the **Divine Truth** not to enforce what I believe, you have access via the internet and books to search for the answers and if only one person who does that and changes their life for the better this will have been worth writing.

There is more to consider regarding the connection. Mediums and clairvoyants connect this solid world with the spirit world. Like it or not, believe it or not, some of them are amazing and are a fantastic help to our police force in solving crimes. They offer great comfort to those who have lost loved ones as well. There are some charlatans out there but many are acting with integrity. Having said that, if you do visit them there is something you should know. I have been informed that spirits have no concept of time as in days, months and years, the 24 hour clock is man made in order for us to keep track of where we are and put order into our lives. Spirit sees the past, present and future all together. So if you are told that you will meet the man or woman of your dreams next Thursday, be suspicious! Also Spiritual mediums and clairvoyants only inform you of one path, only one possible outcome in your future which could change. It all depends on where you are in your life journey now and what you want to happen in your future. As you know as humans we change our minds continuously as to what we want especially when we are young. What they tell you could change.

For example if you suddenly change your job or move house, you may have turned a different corner thus changing your future. You have changed your path and are heading down a new one with new manifestations along the way. I am not saying that these people are wrong, I am just pointing out that not all you are told is carved in stone, you can change things either knowingly or unknowingly. Mediums and clairvoyants help a lot of people and are a strong connection between this dimension and other realms of existence but check out their reputation first before you part with your money.

12. The Bigger Picture

We all have the divine spark within us and together we create the whole. What you see in this world at the moment through the eyes of world media is the result of a fear based society mixed up in a horrid cocktail of humanities negative karma. We are being given the opportunity to repair this damage, to fix the broken souls we have become and to evolve into a higher level of being, with pure intentions in our hearts and minds. I know it sounds too big a task but we have a lot of divine assistance and it is not only possible but necessary for us to change. It must happen; the Divine Plan will be carried out in accordance with God's will. It sounds more difficult than it really is, but we can do it. If we do a little something to help ourselves and pray for Gods Will to be done, that alone will help tremendously.

There is a universal formula that states that the square root of 1% of the population will be enough to change the holographic world we live in, to create a shift in consciousness, that's not many when you think about it. In a world of just under six billion people, it is only about 8000. This is the minimum needed to start the ball rolling in the right direction and change is already upon us. The sky is showing the colours of the rainbow as more light enters the planet. Good things are happening but we are only informed of the bad stuff through the media. More and more of us are waking up and doing our bit to help with the ascension process. Fear is the biggest problem as it keeps mankind trapped in base mentality, causing the fight or flight mode to ignite and people tend to fight. By raising awareness and releasing fear, we can raise our vibration and react from a higher level of consciousness. It is the wise choice really, the changes are happening now and we are all a part of the Divine Plan.

We live in a matrix, a holographic reality that reflects our beliefs, feelings and emotions; our desires, goals and fears are played out for us to learn lessons in order that we can grow. The world acts as a mirror of our consciousness; we are constantly being shown our loves and our deepest fears. The three basic patterns of fear are related to abandonment and separation, low self worth and fear of surrender and trust. These fear based thoughts, desires and beliefs create the negative aspects of not only our daily lives but the reality of the whole planet. The mass of fear based creative energy is the main problem. The only way to rectify the hologram is to remove the fear through self healing, prayer and education based on spiritual growth and to replace that fear with love and compassion. We need to connect to our higher minds and our divinity once more. Maybe you should look up the word **lightworker** on Google (search engine on the internet) and see if you feel a calling to help in some way. Some of us are teachers and others are therapists and practitioners, some just need to look after their own families and be the best examples they can.

It does not matter, what matters is that we wake up and take back our power. That way we control the hologram and not the governments and religious leaders who control the mass consciousness through feeding us fear via the media.

If we want peace, we must be peaceful
If we want trust, we must trust one another
If we want love, we must love ourselves and one another
If we want compassion, we must forgive one another

Have you got it yet? Our world is the creation of our messed up thoughts, feelings and emotions being reflected in a God given hologram based on Karmic consequences. What goes around comes around, to use an old aphorism. You only get out what you put in. Anger creates more anger and fear creates more fearful experiences. We act out all of the situations until we figure it out and change into better people. We need to work through our negative karma and evolve into purer beings of light in this beautiful mystery school called Earth. That is why the planet was created and why we are here, to incarnate into physical bodies in order to learn about sexuality and emotional expression and feelings through experiencing them.

We are spirit in a body that acts as a temporary chariot for our life on this planet, where free will reigns supreme in order to help us to develop. One big experiment really and that may come as a shock to some, but it is true; humanity is an experiment that began way back in Lemuria and Atlantis. We are raising our frequency in order to become enlightened beings once more. That is why there is a need for the complementary and alternative therapies and medicines. Many of us are remembering our old skills and using herbs, crystals, sound, colour and many other healing aids to repair the damage and re-awaken our original 12 strand DNA blueprint.

We will be reconnected with Source and live in peace once more, evolving into the pure souls we once were. We are all ascending and so is Mother Earth as a planet. This does not mean we are all going to float up into heaven. It is about bringing the divine energies down into the planet, bringing heaven down to earth by raising the vibration of ourselves and the planet.

Every living thing on this planet is here to evolve; plants are here to develop mind, animals to develop feelings and man to develop unconditional love and compassion, to become enlightened by finding the path back to Source and Oneness, as it was in Atlantis. Once these new energies are anchored into the planet, we will be living in a new world, free from the confines of the old religious ways, individual spirituality will be the way forward, a one to one relationship with God will be formed. The man made aspect of religion that is based on fear and control will be gone forever. Amen to that.

In Atlantis we were very highly evolved spiritually enlightened souls with amazing healing and telepathic abilities, etc, but it did not leave much scope for growth and evolution was slow because of this. Atlantis fell from grace when a group of high priests became greedy for power, this lead to segregation and fear took form and Atlantis as an experiment was terminated by the great floods.

Few were saved and they carried divine knowledge within their blueprints. The experiment began again, only this time karma was introduced and we have been in a world created by us in a state of cause and effect ever since. The greedier for power mankind became, the more fearful they were and as a result certain chakras were closed down in order for them to survive. This meant that they were vibrating at a much lower frequency. Mankind drifted further from the God Source and less light prevailed as a result. Eventually most people forgot that they were divine sparks of God altogether and the healing and telepathic abilities disappeared as the chakras were closed down. The original 12 strand DNA function shut down, causing the related information and healing capabilities to diminish as a result of becoming more distant from the Divine. It is time to reawaken those skills and THE TIME IS NOW!

13. Dimensions – Physical and non Physical

In general most of us believe that the solid world we see with our eyes, the physical world of time and space, consists of separate elements. This could not be further from the truth. For a start, time and space are not separate entities; they only appear to be that way because of our perception of reality. We look at creation through 3D eyes, see only solid matter and we call it the physical world; solid and separate. We believe it to be unaffected by the past and future, for example, but this is not true.

It is obvious that life has been affected by the past but not so obvious by the future. In the non-physical world there is no time and space; the past, present and the future all exist at the same time, so to speak. They are all happening at the same time. Therefore the present is affected by the past and the future because they coexist in the non-physical realms of creation and a change in one immediately affects the other.

Everything has a level of consciousness and memory, all things are interrelated. In the non-physical world of dimensions, all things are truly connected to one another and therefore the whole, hence Oneness! This being the case, things do not just exist in one dimension at any one time. They exist in other levels of reality, in other dimensions and any one act can have a small or large effect on another level which is removed in time and space. Thus creating change in the physical and the non-physical realms. These events and the effects they may have in our physical world cannot always be explained by our simple laws of physics. This means that there is a lot more to us, the world we live in, the Universe and the whole of creation than we have previously perceived.

We are in general inexperienced in the working and understanding of these "other worlds" or realms of existence and "spiritual dimensions". Because of their immediate effect on our 3D world, maybe now it is time for us to learn more, to communicate and to evolve accordingly into the multidimensional beings of light we truly are. Is it time to break down the barriers and join with our brothers and sisters from these other realms?

First, we need to forget about the old traditional laws of physics and edge more towards the laws of quantum physics and looking at the principals of "probability" and "uncertainty". Quantum mechanics is a theory of many parallel Universes. The difference between one Universe and the next can be so small, maybe only one photon but the reality in that world could be vastly different from ours – it takes all sorts to make a Super Universe!

Reality does not consist of only one dimension but we can in general only see one of them, namely the 3rd dimension unless you are clairvoyant of course or you know how to journey through meditation. Then the possibilities are endless.

I believe that the crystal skulls referred to in the chapter about meditation will help mankind to evolve into higher levels of consciousness and perception; connected on a higher level and capable of interdimensional travel, if only through mediation techniques. Maybe our light body (Merkaba) will take us where we need to go. The Merkaba is our light body which is said to help us travel to other dimensions (through meditation) when we learn to use it. A kind of flying saucer made of light, capable of taking us through portals when we are meditating, and enabling us to explore the matrix of consciousness, something which I consider pretty mind blowing stuff but nevertheless it is easier than one would think. If travelling to other dimensions sounds weird, consider this – we thought that the world was flat 500 years ago! I suggest that you try not to think like a human, you are a light being with amazing super human abilities – you just need to open your mind and believe.

Many people assume that science proves metaphysics to be false; that all things relating to God, heaven, hell and the soul etc do not exist. This is the view of sceptics not scientists. In this age of quantum physics, these invisible entities and energies are believed to exist in other realms and in parallel dimensions. We live in a kind of psychic soup really, just because you cannot see these other beings does not mean that they are not there. There are so many different dimensions and I have listed the main ones below – the following information was taken from The Urantia Book, first published by the Urantia foundation in 1955.

LOCAL UNIVERSE

1st Dimension – Mineral Kingdom
2nd Dimension – Plant Kingdom
3rd Dimension – Humans and Animals
4th Dimension – Astral and Interplanetary Souls
5th Dimension – Extraterrestrial Beings
6th Dimension – Ultra terrestrial Beings

Similar to an Extraterrestrial, the so-called "Ultraterrestrials" are creatures that come from other dimensions, as opposed to other planets.

SUPERUNIVERSE

7th Dimension – Ascended Masters (Parent race to 4D)
8th Dimension – Galactic Masters (Parent race to 5D)
9th Dimension – Multi-Dimensional Over souls (Parent race to 6D)

CENTRAL UNIVERSE

10th Dimension – Timeline Engineers
11th Dimension – Time Lords
12th Dimension – Founders of Universes
13th Dimensions – Central Universe Administration
14th Dimension – Central Universe Headquarters
15th Dimension – Paradise Trinity

It would appear from this list that there is quite a lot going on out there!

14. Angels and Ascended Masters

We are very fortunate to have these amazing light beings in this dimension helping us through the changes on the planet, as we move closer to 2012 and the evolutionary change to higher levels of consciousness. These beings are by our side day and night helping us and guiding us. More recently, the unicorn energy has arrived, these beautiful beings of light leave a feather as a calling card, just like the Angels; they are full of light and are more than willing to help us to become enlightened. But we need to ask for help and guidance as light beings will only intervene in free will, in a life threatening situation. If we do not ask for their help they cannot help us.

Before I go any further, I would like to say that I have searched to try and find out exactly what will be happening in 2012. There are many stories, and nobody really knows. Some predict doom and gloom. Please ignore them, remember that we have the ability to co-create with the Universe. Prophecy can change; all prophecy is accurate but only at that point in time. Therefore all prophecy can be rewritten. If we worry, we will damage the Divine Plan and according to the book of Urantia, there is definitely a Divine Plan and we are all a part of it. The best thing to do is to have faith that the Universe has a Divine Plan and will create the perfect world. We should manifest this by praying that the Divine Plan is implemented in accordance with Divine will.

Angels can help with the simplest of things from finding a parking space to helping you put together a dinner party. They love to help and you can show your appreciation by playing them beautiful music and singing for them. I do this often and it makes me feel very emotional and connected to my divine helpers. We can also ask the Ascended Masters to help us. My favourites are Archangel Michael, Archangel Gabriel, Archangel Uriel and Archangel Raphael. Whenever I am a working, I call upon these mighty Archangel's and ask them to stand at the four points north, south, east and west to guide and protect me as I work. Archangel Michael, in my eyes is the heart and soul of Crystal Ki Healing. He helps with the tie cutting, which is essential to clearing negative energies, entities, ET's and releasing us from negative attachments.

It is possible to write to some of the Ascended Masters, namely the Karmic Board, twice a year for dispensation and sponsorship.

The Karmic Board are an eight member board of Ascended Masters who dispense justice to the souls on this planet. They consist of the following....

The Great Divine Director
The Goddess of Liberty
Lady Master Nada
Elohim Cyclopea
Pallas Athena, twin flame of the Maha Chohan
Lady Master Portia, St Germain's twin flame
Quan Yin, Goddess of Mercy
The Dhyani Buddha Vairochana

We all know these Masters as we have passed before them many times before and after every incarnation on this planet. They are there to adjudicate Karma, mercy and judgement. These Masters have complete unrestricted access to our Akashic records. These records contain all information about us and the whole of creation, a kind of etheric library which we can access through meditation.

We can write to them twice a year to give gratitude, seek divine guidance asking for resolutions to our earthly problems and for dispensation. We can also ask for help and sponsorship with our earthly missions. This mighty board meet on New Years Eve and on the 4th July at the Royal Teton Retreat. This is when the petitions are read and dispensations awarded as deserved.

Every six months we are given the opportunity to look at our lives, make offerings to God, surrender our bad habits, etc. It is best to under promise and over deliver in our petitions. We can do this by writing a letter to the Karmic board as follows....

The letter must be hand written during the fourteen days before the meeting at the retreat. Include your offering to God, what you are willing to resolve in your short comings and what you are requesting dispensation or sponsorship with. Keep a copy of the letter and consecrate (meaning to set aside with divine intent) the original by creating a small alter or sacred space. On the said date, ask your Guardian Angel to take the letter to the Karmic Board on your behalf. They will take the information not the physical letter; you need to burn the letter after you have requested your Angel to take it to the Retreat. Then it is a matter of having faith and seeing what happens next. You can meditate and ask to be taken to speak to Lady Master Nada or any other member of the Board you feel drawn to and ask if your requests are to be granted.

15. New Energies and Transitional Problems

This planet is being flooded with new solar, cosmic and galactic energies even the magnetic grid around the planet is altering to suit the new earth frequencies, we are all being upgraded to a higher frequency, many of us can feel the shift as it happens. Energy is constantly changing and we must go with the flow and incorporate these new energies into our energy fields as we evolve with Mother Earth into higher levels of consciousness, this is referred to as ascension or the ascension process.

Most of us can feel the process taking place, though some of us are suffering as a consequence of the process with illness and tiredness being the main problems. These are referred to as transitional problems as we are all in transit, becoming purer higher light beings and changing on a cellular level. As our consciousness rises it can bring emotional and physical discomfort as we anchor our soul into our physical selves. Our internal organs become less dense as they no longer hold and express the emotions in them that they did easily generations ago. We are less tolerant of situations that we once were. If we resist change the soul will allow us to become ill until we work through our issues and release them completely.

The most common transitional problem is tiredness; this is because of the changes at cellular level, as the cells change and become less dense the human body systems have more work to do processing these changes and we become tired as a result. The best action is to rest and eat highly nutritional foods. As aches and pains come and go, doctors cannot find a reason for these problems and people can have palpitations as the heart chakra realigns itself to the higher energies. Psychic abilities are increasing as we awaken dormant DNA previously referred to as junk DNA. There is also a slight increase in the brain size which can cause headaches although not everyone suffers these transitional conditions.

It is common to see the numbers 11:11 in ratio form when going through transition (moving from one level of consciousness to the next) and this is time to take extra care with eating properly, getting adequate rest and retreating if necessary. I always feel wide open when I am between levels and the transition is heartfelt. I can feel very emotional as I release old energies and belief systems, but once they have been released I feel invigorated and I state clearly to the Universe that I accept this new level of consciousness. It is important to make that statement in order to fully anchor in your new level of consciousness and the energy it brings with it. I do this to anchor myself mentally into this new level of consciousness, having not bothered to say so in the past, I noticed I stayed in transition much longer than required, which meant I felt vulnerable and lost as if I was neither here nor there.

When I am in transition I feel far more sensitive to all energies that are around me and to be honest the best thing I find to do at these times is to stay at home and keep clearing out old energies and working through what needs to be released.

As we reach higher levels of consciousness and we change on a cellular level, we become closer to Source and therefore more powerful co creators. As we raise our vibration, it is important that we realise that we have more power and to use that power wisely. Not being ready for the higher levels would be like giving the keys of a Ferrari to a learner driver, a disaster in the making. In order to reach the top, one must accept this new responsibility and hence a new way of life.

There are many beings here to help us, the Angels being some of them. When I first woke up to the changes taking place on the planet and healing, my Angels became my new best friends, in particular Archangel Michael, he has always been around me and protects me when I need him. My Guardian Angel has been a great help to me over the years and I am truly grateful, we are on first name terms and he was the first contact I had with these Divine Beings.

The main Archangels are the representatives of the seven rays of life and they retreat at a certain special places on the planet. Ascended Masters were once in human form and gained mastery over the material planes, they balanced at least 51% of their negative karma and fulfilled their Divine Plan; they are God-like and united in their own presence (God-self).

By simply saying out loud or in your mind the following words, you can call upon these Wise Beings for help.

Affirm (3 Times)......I call upon the Ascended Masters to help and guide me today.

If you know the name of a particular Master or Archangel, just insert their name. Say the affirmation 3 times and they will come, they always do. All of these beings are here with us, you do not have to be special to connect with them, just have an open mind and an open heart.

16. Atlantis, DNA and Indigo Children

It is recorded that in Atlantis many different types of spiritual beings from different corners of the universe incarnated into a human template. There was no illness, no sadness, everybody was pure, and therefore there was no karma. People traded with one another and there was plenty for everybody. This was before the fall from grace. It only took a few of the high priests to make some wrong choices, and the beautiful perfection was ruined. Before this we were all healers, we were all telepathic.

We were capable of inter-dimensional travel; we had super human strengths and abilities. We also had twelve strands of DNA as opposed to the two strands of DNA, we were reduced to. These priests interfered with the brain, splitting it into two sections, in order to stop our telepathy. They did not want us to know what they were thinking and the brain was split into the two halves of logic and intuition.

After a while, telepathic powers ceased to work correctly and this is when verbal language evolved and people became divided into groups. The once perfect place was now contaminated with fear and other negative emotions; we began to lose the ability to use the twelve strands of DNA to their full capacity. Atlantis became so contaminated that it had to be destroyed. The experiment had failed!

Most of the people on this planet are said to originate from other worlds, other planets. This may sound crazy, but nevertheless I believe it to be true. Many of us have stellar origins as either star people or Angels and have been born at this time for a reason; that reason is to help with the current changes and the Ascension process. We are in the process of reactivating the original twelve strands of DNA. The ten strands that were disconnected, were unravelled and implants were put in to stop them reconnecting. These implants can be removed by competent healers or through prayer.

The repercussions had a detrimental affect on the pineal gland, the pituitary gland and the hypothalamus gland, and these glands have shrunken in size from non use. This can easily be corrected by reactivation of our original blueprint through healing meditation. We are gradually reconnecting and rebuilding DNA. When the numbers 11:11 are brought to your attention, your DNA is upgrading. The 11:11 is a signal or code that triggers changes in your DNA, these changes have been happening for years and none of us now have only the original two strands, we have all been upgraded to higher levels.

There have been children born throughout the history of humanity to help raise the vibration of the planet that have more than two strands of DNA active. They are very intelligent, loving and amazing children that are being mistakenly diagnosed with A.D.D., A.D.H.D. and Asperger Syndrome - these are Autistic Spectrum Disorders. I discuss them further in the next chapter.

17. Autistic Spectrum Disorders

There are two ways of looking at Autistic Spectrum Disorders (ASD), Attention Deficit Hyperactivity Disorder (ADHD), Attention Deficit Disorder (ADD) and Asperger Syndrome.

Firstly, the medical professions view which refers to poor social skills, obsessive behaviours and hyperactivity problems, etc. And that is all I want to say about it because it is labelling children and adults with the mental disability badge which really annoys me and them.

Secondly, the fact that these children are not disabled they are highly gifted and talented individuals that have been born at a higher frequency than normal and are therefore more spiritually evolved than most. Some are very much more evolved and they can be clairvoyant, clairsentient, clairaudient etc. They can also be telepathic with immense psychic powers and natural healing abilities. Some of these children can turn lights on and off without touching them and recharge batteries with their minds. According to age they are referred to as either Indigo children, Crystal children or Rainbow children, depending on when they were born and the colours in their energy field.

Indigo children tend to be the warrior spirit and will clear the way for the more delicate and sensitive Crystal children. The Rainbow children are such highly evolved souls and they actually look like angels with an amazing amount of light around them; their wisdom can be profound as if they have lived many previous lives and some can remember them.

My son, who was labelled with Aspergers Syndrome and born in 1992, is a typical Indigo child. I had a fabulous pregnancy and gained only 7lb over the nine months, I was eating properly, the birth was straight forward, and I remember his first word at only eight months old when he pointed to a light bulb in my parents' house and said "Light", uncanny really considering we are both light workers.

He was 18 months old when I began to realise that something was not quite normal, he would line up shoes, pebbles and toys in perfect straight lines, constantly. He was a nightmare to feed at meal times, and it would often end in tears with both of us upset; he just did not want to eat. Perhaps even at that delicate young age, he knew he could survive on light. However, I was brought up on three course dinners, and if he did not eat his meals, he must be sick. Meal times were dreaded by me.

By the time he started pre-school at three, it was clear to me that something was wrong. He was fine at home but when he was with other children he became hyperactive and sometimes aggressive. He could not sit at the table with other children in class; he was instead underneath it, or distracting others. Trips to school to discuss his behaviour with his teacher became common practice. I would cry so much because I did not know what to do. At home my son was an angel, but at school be became the class clown and a constant distraction, we were told that he had behavioural problems.

His father did not see the problem and even the family said that he was fine and that I had no patience with him; I have repaired the emotional damage it did to me, but it was heart breaking at the time. I just wanted someone to fix him and take the problem away, what a terrible way to think of your child. I blamed myself and the guilt I felt was crippling.

My mother was an enormous help, she would baby sit every Saturday, and I am forever grateful for that as I really needed the space, as much as I loved him, it could be hard work at times. When he was seven years old and I was almost at breaking point, his teacher called us into school to discuss his behaviour again. She said that she thought he was showing signs of ASD (Autistic Spectrum Disorder). A year later he was diagnosed with Aspergers Syndrome. To be honest it was a relief, as I was beginning to think I was going crazy. He was statemented with special needs and awarded nineteen hours teaching assistance per week, in mainstream education: not that this did him a lot of good as the School he went to decided to split the nineteen hours over a two week period and I did not find this out for nearly four years, by which time the damage to his education had been done.

I read the medical information and then eventually I went to the book shop to find out the spiritual information after being told about Indigo children by a friend. I found a calmness come over me because at least I could work with this now, and I knew what it was.

When he was 10 years old, I read about Crystal and Indigo children on the internet and this was very informative. I now understood him better and viewed him as a spiritual being and not a problem child. I decided the main thing I needed to do with him was to get him grounded and I took him to a crystal shop. Once there he picked all of the crystals he required that would help him. They were onyx, tiger eye and hematite, all grounding crystals connected to the base chakra. They really began to work and he was much calmer, which meant I was too. It was a massive turning point and the beginning of my spiritual awakening and guidance towards becoming a practitioner. This was when I discovered he was clairvoyant and very telepathic, we grew closer and developed a relationship with our angels, we were much more tuned in to one another and grew closer as a result.

As I learnt about autistic issues, I realised that I had them too; I knew I was not quite the same as other people, but at last I knew why now. That was when my abilities became apparent and since then I have never looked back.

I now accepted the fact that Autistic Spectrum Disorders were a gift and not a mental disability.

If you have a child with one of these so-called disorders the best thing I can advise you to do is to get them grounded, take them to a complimentary therapist or to a crystal shop (let them choose the crystals), read about Crystal, Indigo and Rainbow children and find out more about their abilities and focus on the positive aspects before you do them harm by labelling them as mentally disabled, which is what the medical profession have done.
My son hated being labelled and still does. He knows he is gifted now and that has made a big difference to his self esteem. These children are SPECIAL as in fantastic and talented!

It is important to speak to these children in a correct manner as they do not understand abstract or ambiguous language (slang). I once had a teacher tell me that my son was being rude as when he was told that he needed to pull his socks up (meaning to work a bit harder), he looked down at them and replied, "They are up". He took many things very literally and this was distressing as we needed to explain and teach him what certain sayings meant constantly. It was like teaching him a whole new language.

These children also do not respond to commands and it is important to give them a choice by asking them to do something rather than telling them. Telling someone to carry out a task is interfering with free will and is not spiritually correct behaviour; these children are very wise and spiritually evolved and need to be treated accordingly.

My son is nearly 16 years old and is so laid back and grounded now. People that see him now are surprised at this calmness and some even ask what I have done to him, of course I reply "nothing" and just tell them that he is grounded now. He is a much calmer, happier child and is a pleasure to be around, I am so blessed.

18. The Conscious and the Sub-conscious Mind

In order to break and release old habits, negative belief patterns and behaviours and so on, we need to clear the programming from the subconscious mind. The subconscious part of the mind has six main functions; they are to act as a memory bank, to form the seat of our imagination and of our emotions. The subconscious regulates our heartbeat and breathing etc. It holds onto the patterns and beliefs and it is also responsible for the drive and motivation of the energy we have.

It responds to repetition and can be altered by using affirmations, one of my favourites being "I am healthy, wealthy and wise" which seems to cover all areas really.

The logical mind is responsible for reasoning and logical behaviour, you use your logical mind to move your hand to pick up a book or to choose a place you want to go and eat, or to add and subtract for example. By consciously repeating an affirmation we can train the subconscious mind to accept the affirmation as a belief. Things can go wrong for us when we are repeatedly told we are stupid or that we are not good enough or that we are fat or ugly, etc. This can programme our sub-conscious mind into believing these comments and they become parts of us, stored in our memory banks, they can lead to all kinds of mental and emotional hang ups which can eventually filter through to manifest as an actual physical illness, even cancer apparently.

In a positive light, we can train the sub-conscious mind to act as an auto-pilot for us. Take learning to ride a bike. At first it is difficult and we must learn to concentrate on more than one thing at once and all working in unison, peddling, steering, and looking where you are going. However, after a short while with some repetition and practice we can jump on the bike and ride it steadily, without even having to think about it, with the subconscious doing most of the work for us. The same goes for driving a car, we do not have to think every time we change gear or turn the steering wheel, it just comes naturally via the subconscious programming as a result of practise.

It is possible to reprogram negative beliefs and behaviour and it usually takes around 21 days to programme the mind. And re-programming using clearing techniques is said to also take 21 days.

The subconscious mind is in control of our emotions such as fear and anxiety and all automatic emotional responses. Fear and anxiety are energy as is everything in existence and can therefore be removed by tie cutting and space clearing (see chapter on Tie Cutting). This means that using the techniques in this book, it is possible to remove fear and anxiety in one or two sessions. I have had fantastic results with anxious clients by removing the fear and anxiety.

Try to see your mind as a computer; your automatic emotional responses are programmes as are all of your belief systems. For example, if you repeatedly saw your father get angry and violent when you were younger, your programming could respond in the same way to stressful situations, or make you so frightened, that you just run away altogether, either way it is not the correct response to anger.

Anger needs to be released from the system as it may damage the liver if it is repressed; therefore the best thing to do is release the anger in a controlled manner. So if you need to lash out, punch the pillow, go for a brisk walk or count to ten and breathe out the anger.

By feeding your subconscious mind with the correct programming you can release old habits and belief systems and fix many personality problems. The conscious and subconscious minds form a team and when working and programmed correctly they are absolutely brilliant resulting in our emotions and our views on life being grounded and stable.

I used tie cutting to help me to reprogram my belief that I needed cigarettes. I would visualise the cigarette about five meters away from me and cut ties with it, stating this sentence – "I cut and release you with love and peace, I am totally free". It is important

69

to say this sentence as it releases the energy as well. Whenever I felt like a cigarette I would cut ties with it until I no longer wanted one. I did manage to kick the habit.

I did the same to release the belief that I thought romantic love was a trap, although this time I visualised a disc of Crystal Ki light moving through my body and a net of light taking that belief system away, I could actually see a heart and a cage being lifted away in my minds eye in the net. The chapter on Tie Cutting and Space Clearing explains this technique and how to perform it in more detail.

19. The Mass Consciousness Creates our World

The collective consciousness of our thoughts and feelings creates the world we live in. We are the world; we are God, every living thing in existence is part of God. The thing that takes us away from that level of consciousness is fear. When fear is allowed to control our thoughts and feelings it runs wild creating the negative aspects of the violent world we can all see today. We are responsible; through ignorance we have created this mess, the good news is we can repair it, not by battling to change the old one but by creating a new one and forcing the old to become obsolete. The only way to achieve this is to release the fear and replace it with peace. Peaceful hearts and minds create a peaceful world. It is not politicians and religious leaders who will create peace, it is us! We are the creative mass of consciousness and therefore the Power! It is all to do with our light frequency or vibration and the holographic make up of the reality we live in.

Television, the internet and the media pump us full of the negative information and news keeping us in a state of fear. When we are fearful, we are weak and a low frequency or vibration. The higher your frequency the more powerful a creator you become Our God given creative powers are therefore manipulated as a result of negative input. We all have the divine spark within and we all have the ability to create our lives, to live in a beautiful peaceful world. Bad news keeps the base chakra in a fight or flight mode of thought thus keeping the whole planet trapped in a negative state of existence. Paedophilia, corruption and so called terrorists groups are fed to people and children as they sit in front of the television having dinner in the evening. This information can be really soul destroying. Your soul is pure and deserves pure input so why feed it this rubbish?

If you must watch television, try watching pre-recorded films and DVD's as they are less damaging than live television. I would also recommend films that avoid violence and sex or any subject that makes you feel sad, or disturbs you. I would recommend trying to avoid the news, television and newspapers for a week if not for good and to see how much better you feel. Although it is fair to say that some may struggle with that as they are addicted to bad news. Tuning in to watch a news program can be filling your living space with fear and disharmony; the other option is listening to beautiful music or even silence, all of which are healthier, the choice is yours.

I have some very bright friends who insist on reading newspapers and think they are essential to modern life and believe that they are not being fooled because they read between the lines so to speak. The people who write the papers write the stuff between the lines, to influence the minds of intelligent people as well.

Wake up! They have still had your attention on the subject of war and famine, etc and your thoughts have been adding to the mass negativity as you read it, even whilst you were reading between the lines. For the time you were reading about negative incidences you have been a low frequency creator amidst the mass consciousness because it is difficult to read doom and gloom and send out positive energy a the same time, unless you know how to transmute your energy as you create it and only an enlightened few know how to do that. This being the case even the jolly happy souls who read between the lines have to take responsibly for the state of the world. We all need to act and create the world we intend our children and grandchildren to live in and then take action to make it happen.

We allow ourselves to be pumped full of drugs like penicillin some of which no longer work because we eat them in the meat we buy from the supermarkets. The cattle are injected as soon as they are born. We are bound to become immune sooner or later. Pharmaceutical companies are making a fortune out of our illness and dis-ease. I imagine that they are not too keen on complementary medicine either as it loses them money when we consult natural health care practitioners. We can live without chemical drugs if we choose to eat well, be happy, exercise and live a balanced lifestyle. We are all beings of light with amazing self-healing abilities as part of our creative make-up.

We are being contaminated with the food that we eat, due to the additives and preservatives. Our water supply has fluoride in it which was used during the war to keep prisoners of war docile as it suppresses the will centres in the mind. We are being drugged constantly and manipulated constantly. It is time to stop being lambs to the slaughter and act now. Feed your families fresh organic food and the supermarkets will lower the price of it so everyone can afford it. We owe it to ourselves and children to feed them the best.

These chemicals lower our frequency and suppress our psychic and healing abilities, as well as poisoning us and keeping us sick and reliant on the pharmaceutical companies. They make money, we stay sick and die! Some how it does not feel real but it is and it is up to all of us to take control of our lives and do something about it. Maybe you should investigate the dangers of chemicals in your diet and realise that you could be killing yourself and your children. By simply eating better you could prolong your life (organic food if possible, nothing processed or frozen pre-packed foods, avoiding additives and preservatives). Maybe take some exercise as even a twenty minute brisk walk a day will help. By doing these things and drinking pure water (6 to 8 glasses per day) you will feel a lot better and raise your vibration.

Try to take a few deep breaths regularly and let the life force flow into your hearts and minds. Rather than sitting in front of the television to have dinner, sit around a table and talk with the family and turn the TV off, maybe go for a walk afterwards.

Try letting go of fear, as it attracts fearful situations to you, try to change the way you think and be more positive. Take back control of the collective consciousness of the masses and let our purer minds create the world we live in, as together we can all help to build a perfect world.

We have the power – but we must be pro-active, if only in a small way, it all helps, we are all ONE. All we need to do is bring more light into the planet. This will show us the Divine Truth. Ask God to flush out the corruption, to bless and purify the politicians and the planet in general, allowing us to create a purer way of life. The life you would like for yourself and your children.

The Universal energies are here to help but we need to ask for that help and we all need to do our bit. We can change the balance of light and dark on our planet with a little input from a lot of the people. Taking more care of your health and well being is all you need to do.

It is important to know that the people who appear to be in control of our creative energy are living in fear themselves, even though they probably do not even realise it. People who crave money have fear of lack, people who crave power are fearful of losing control. Allocating blame is not the answer here, we need to educate and enlighten ourselves in order to move forward, to forgive not fight. Take Ghandi for example; Ghandi was more powerful than the British Empire because of his light and spiritual level of consciousness; he was closer to God and hence more powerful than the Empire as a result. When we move closer to that Divine Source of love we raise not only our vibration but the vibration of the whole planet and help to make a better life for all concerned. The more light we bring into our world the brighter it will shine on the darkness, the corrupt will be moved peacefully out with light and compassion, not aggression and control. It is important to be pro peace not anti war, being anti war means you are giving your energy to war not peace.

If we are aggressive, we only add more darkness and keep things as they are. If you see the corrupt officials as lost children, just as God would, it would be easier to let go of their short comings and to fix it the only way we can, with compassion and wisdom, peace not war. Try not to see them as sinners but as having obstacles blocking them from that Divine Source. When we ask God to help those who are doing wrong, he immediately sends them higher frequency energy which will help them to get closer to him. We have no right to judge, Only God has that right and he chooses forgiveness first every time. Forgiveness is essential to the evolution of the planet.

We are all souls on our own journey through this mystery school and we are all at different levels. Everything is happening for a reason and within divine time limits. The corrupt are there through fear based thought forms and their lesson is to recognise and correct that. It is not for us to judge! But we can take back our control and our energy, our power to create and use it in more positive ways thus diminishing the shadows that hold the world in this low frequency reality.

We now have the opportunity to raise our vibration thus raising the vibration of the whole planet and all life on it. There is a Divine Plan at work and it will be carried out in accordance with Divine Will because the Universe cannot let mankind destroy this planet, as it would have a knock on effect for all of creation not just our galaxy. Mother Earth is on the path to ascension and so are we, whether we like it or not, and some don't like it. I say, "Bring it on!"

The Angels and other beings of light are here to help us and guide us along the way. If you find it hard to believe in and accept these divine helpers try to understand the science of creation and the fact that you are creating this world and your future now with everything you say, do, think and feel. So why not start thinking purer thoughts and create a beautiful world free from fear based behaviour. You do not need to be specific (your ego self is not wise enough to choose a perfect world – your perfect world might be full of super models or pink fluffy bunnies, perfect for you maybe but not for the rest of us).

You need only think of a world that is full of unconditional love, trust, peace and compassion. "May Gods will be done, Amen" saying this statement alone helps to do the trick. You may like to say it when you wake in the morning and again when you go to bed at night, it could have a huge impact in bringing heaven down to earth if more of us say this simple sentence regularly. A little prayer goes a long way when said by a lot of people.

Learning to connect to your higher self and to meditate can help; it does not mean you need to sit in the lotus position like some kind of Buddha for hours on end. You can connect to your higher self by simply visualising a line of light (this acts as a communication cable) from a gold sphere (this represents your higher self) about 12 inches above your head coming down into your mind connecting you with your higher mind. If you set the intention to connect to your higher self you will be connected. Your higher self will always guide you. All you need to do is to ask the question and wait for the answers. If you hear a voice that gives you a message to do something bad, then there is a good chance you have a negative spirit attached to you. My advice would be to ignore it and demand it leaves you alone. If it does not leave, you can carry out a tie cutting as explained later in this book or you may need to find a spiritual healer who can move it on for you.

You can meditate while sitting in the comfort of your own home or walking in the park. It is easy and anyone can do it, and what is more, it's free. You could be cooking a meal or painting your home, it does not matter as long as you feel lost in the moment and relaxed, and the usual mind chatter is ignored or has ceased during your medative session. It is all food for the soul.

20. The Map of Consciousness

The Map of Consciousness was created by a brilliant spiritual teacher called Dr David Hawkins in order to calibrate where we are on the spiritual path in relation to consciousness and the journey back to source, and total self realisation.

As we move forward and release old issues and learn more about spirituality and ascension, we progress through various areas stated in the map of consciousness such as love and wisdom. The emotions we feel and the processes we go through during those changes are listed, and the God view and life view we feel as a result of certain levels of attainment.

The lowest level in the map is shame followed by guilt, apathy, fear, anxiety, anger then pride; all of these states of consciousness make the person feel weak. They are all low frequency. Once we transcend these levels there is a breakthrough considered the level of integrity and courage which calibrates at 200 on the scale. People at this level and above become much stronger and have more spiritual power. 500 is the level of real love. Jesus, Buddha and Krishna calibrated at 1000, this is the highest level the human nervous system can cope with or so we are lead to believe, I am aware of people that do calibrate above this level.

Ghandi was at 760, Sir Albert Einstein and Sir Isaac Newton were at 499, and they were stuck at the level of intellect. The book a Course in Miracles Work Book, tested at 600, the music of Louis Armstrong at 590. The higher the level, the closer to God and to self-realisation we become, life becomes easier as we release our emotions and keep moving towards pure consciousness. Eventually your whole life is just pure peace as you reach the 600 level, the level of unconditional love. According to Dr Hawkins approximately 50% of people who reach this 600 level leave the planet; they do so of their own free will. The rest of us choose to stay behind and help with the ascension process.

This map is fully explained in the book called Power vs. Force by Dr David Hawkins. His audio programme entitled the Highest Level of Enlightenment is also very interesting. Even if your conscious mind cannot understand all of the information, your soul will understand every word, thus raising your vibration by just listening to it.

You can test all sorts of things by doing K-testing which stands for Kinesiology testing. This was how the map of consciousness was created by Dr David Hawkins and his colleagues.

Kinesiology Testing

It is necessary to do these tests with another person. The two of you should face one another a few feet apart; the tester places their right hand on the shoulder of the person being tested. With the test person putting out their right arm out to the side parallel to the ground and at 90 degrees to the body, they close their eyes while the tester presses down two fingers on the wrist of the test subject whilst saying "resist". The test subject should be able to resist the pressure easily whilst the tester keeps doing this.

Next the subject is asked to think of something they love and something that makes them happy, the tester then does the same two fingers on the wrist exercise, pressing down, and the subject should be able to resist easily.

The subject is then asked to think of something that makes them unhappy or sad, and the same process of two fingers on the wrist and pressing down is applied, however this time the test subject is unable to resist and the arm will go weak and move downwards.

By doing these tests both the tester and the test subject should get good ideas as to what gives a good strong positive response, or a weak or non-response. The principal about this test is that truth and integrity have an anabolic positive effect on your field of consciousness; whist false non-integrous things will have a catabolic negative impact on the field.

Another way to K test is for the test subject to hold something to be tested in their left hand holding to their solar plexus just below their heart and in the centre of their ribcage. The tester states for example apples are positive resist, to test if apples are good for the subject. Pressure is applied to the subject's wrist just as before. If they are good for the subject, the arm will not move down. It is important to give declarations rather than ask questions. You can use this to test foods, flower remedies, music, colours etc, whatever you like.

It is important to detach from the outcome, and remove all watches and jewellery etc. It is also important that both of you calibrate above 200 which is the level of integrity to get good clear results. The results may be affected by the test subject if something negative is in their energy centres, these can be temporarily removed by using the thymus thump. The thymus gland is located behind the sternum just beneath the clavicle; it is the higher heart chakra situated between the throat chakra and the heart chakra. If you thump firmly on the thymus three times (without hurting the person of course) and say "ha, ha, ha" three times (nine in all) this should improve the energetic flow and give an uplifting feeling.

21. Mental and Emotional Causes of Disease

In order to heal we first need to intend to get better and some people would rather take potions and pills rather than face the repressed emotions that healing can bring to the surface. Others enjoy the attention that they receive as a result of being ill; this can mean that their inner child is craving love or that they are just lonely. Others may be stuck in a victim mentality level of consciousness which means that they are happy moaning and blaming the world for their illness or problems as it takes the responsibility for correcting the situation off of their shoulders. However whatever the case may be, it is important to realise that illness can teach us so much, usually the hard way unfortunately, through pain and suffering.

Your soul chooses certain diseases in order to get your attention and point you in the right direction. Some people prefer surgery rather than changing their negative thinking or behaviour and that is their choice.

We can only heal when we are ready and we can only help others when they ask us for help unless we ask permission from their higher selves of course. Some people sit back and expect God or a doctor to heal them but by giving all of your healing process to your doctor, you are actually giving away your power.

We need to participate in our own healing process and hope that we are on track, thanking God every day for our health and wellbeing as we begin to heal is a good start. The Native Americans thought that evoking the help of the lizard would help with the regeneration of the physical body and hence the healing process. It is also important to have hope as hopelessness can cause us to shut down completely and cause terminal illness in itself. Hope means we have some kind of faith and where there is faith there is light and this is essential to healing, as we are made of light energy after all.

People with hope and a positive mental outlook will get better much quicker than those without these attributes. The helpless ones will either get worse or take longer to get better and feeling sorry for yourself will only take away your positive healing power.

In order to heal it is important to remove the energy blocks from the body. These are usually repressed mental and emotional feelings and belief systems, all of which are masses of energy which have formed to create an ailment over a period of time. They are negative programming and all energy can be moved and transformed. Hatred, anger, fears, jealously, etc, can all be released and replaced with purer energy.

Most people are scared of facing these repressed emotions but once they do they usually find that it was not as bad as they thought it was going to be, and can move on with their lives with a sense of peace and freedom as well as a healthy body. Miracles happen everyday; it's just that the people who perform them do not feel the need to shout about it.

There are many ways to find help and healing; the human body is a self healing machine once pointed in the right direction, we can regenerate on many levels. Think how quickly the skin heals after a nasty case of sunburn, or how a cut finger or limb knits and heals together. We see scars heal and stitches removed after operations only days after we have had them, it is miraculous how quickly we can heal.

Once you realise that the body self heals, you just need to find some way of helping yourself to release the repressed negative and emotional memories that can cause problems in the physical and then you will be well on your way to health and wellbeing again.

Ask for help from your angels or guides or whatever you believe in and find the right therapist, ask your friends. Make sure your therapist realises that they are only a guide and not in control of the healing. I never heal my clients; I help them to heal themselves by moving the blocks. A therapist can open the door but you are the one that walks through it and a little faith goes a long long way.

There are many different reasons for illness and disease, but listed here are a few of the most common ones that I have come across.

Migraines – These can be related to frustration or an overload of information, also repressed rage. They are also a way of taking time out for some people and possibly in a few cases, attention seeking. Sugar can cause migraines, other causes can be anger and perfectionism, and these are all factors that should be addressed.

Ears – Problems with your ears relate to not wanting to hear what is going on in the world; we are shutting down to things that we don't like the sound of.

Earaches, especially in young children can mean that they are not happy in their environment. Deafness is about not wanting to listen to other people and not wanting to hear what they are saying. Tinnitus is related to not expressing enough self love as your soul shuts the outside world out as it forces us to focus upon ourselves.

Neck – Problems here can reflect in being inflexible to life as the head and body become separated leading us to become materialist and shallow. A blocked chakra can also cause throat problems, with stiff necks being about restricted vision and not seeing all sides of the story (narrow mindedness). Stress can also lead to neck problems.

Back – Upper back and shoulder problems are related to needing some emotional support, with feeling burdened and carrying the weight of the world on our shoulders. Problems in the middle back can be related to guilt, fear and anger which can get trapped in the kidneys and cause pain. The lower back is usually around the location of the sacral chakra (just below the naval) which is the emotional centre and can mean emotionally holding on to unexpressed emotions that need to be let out, and also worries about money. Problems with the root or the base of the spine can also relate to not being grounded or even the will to live (or rather the lack of it).

Stomach – Problems here seem to stem from who or what we can stomach. This is the point of power in the body, lack of focus results if this area is blocked. It is about digesting reality and feelings. Fear also causes problems in this area.

Ulcers – These are related to fear, and not feeling we are good enough, low self-esteem and other self worth issues.

Bladder – Infections here are connected to holding in painful emotions and being "peed off" with what is going on around us.

Prostrate – Problems in this area are related to issues with self-worth and sexual prowess and is much more common in older men than younger men.

Knees – Problems here can indicate issues with authority or the fear of moving forward and it can also indicate emotional problems. Knee pain can be due to blocked energy centres causing problems with grounding. Other issues are that we are too proud or resistance in moving into a new direction.

Gout – This can relate to holding on to negative emotions, thought patterns and attitudes. This can be due to a lack of good blood flow related to lack of love flowing through us and hence not enough energy to balance the negative feelings

Cancer – This can be related to negative emotional and mental accumulation in the affected area amongst many other things. It appears to be the manifestation of years of negative feelings and emotions on a deep level and an accumulation in the affected area. Take breast cancer for example, this can be related to self love or rather the lack of it. Women have more problems with self love than men do, because women are often seen as someone's wife, mother, daughter, etc, instead of being seen as a woman in their own right and being seen as themselves. Being all these things to all these people and constantly giving closes us to giving to ourselves which can lead to lymph tissue problems. These are connected to the thymus gland, the higher heart chakra. Blocked lymph nodes are common and can be cleared by having a lymphatic massage, then you need to love yourself and I mean really love yourself.

It is not selfish can be life saving and it is essential. After all you want to live long enough to see your children grow up and to be around for your family, so you will not only be doing yourself a favour by putting yourself first, but you will be prolonging your life and that will benefit them. If you do not love yourself your thymus chakra can become blocked thus blocking the underarm lymph's which can affect the lymphatic system causing disease. Self love and creative expression are such an important part of being a woman or for a man for that matter, we all need to love and accept ourselves more and here a few ways we can do it.

a. Treat yourself to some flowers or goodies every now and then.
b. Take some time out to do exactly what you want on a regular basis.
c. Have a glass of wine now but remember the first glass can be healthy, whereas the second glass cancels out the first and the third glass is toxic.
d. Say "NO" more often, especially to your family otherwise they can take, take, take if you let them, I am sure you realise that.
e. Delegate some of the chores, you are not a servant.
f. Have a weekend off, go away in the country every now and then, they will survive without you, honest.
h. Ask for help when you need it instead of trying to do it all by yourself. It is important to stop giving all the time, this allows for the balance of us to be able to receive – give and take. Most of all do not feel guilty about having some me time, we all deserve it. Try not to worry about your family, as it only sends them negative energy which will do them and you more harm than good. Look after yourself more and you will live a much longer and happier life.

I once read a little book by Mike George called "The 7 Aha's of Highly Enlightened Souls" where he wrote the following which proves that happiness can heal disease, maybe even cancer. In this little book he stated that research scientists had taken seratonin, a chemical hormone produced in the human brain when we are happy and placed it in a test tube with cancer cells in. The cancer cells were killed immediately. When they were asked why they had not tried this before, they replied that there were a million chemicals that needed to be tested and they had only just got round to trying seratonin.

When we look at common ailments then think about the mental, emotional or even spiritual causes, we can see how important it is to release our fears, speak our truths and to put ourselves first (not in a conceited way) and to love ourselves in order to be loved.

Not speaking our truth means that we hold emotions and negativity in and this can lead to all kinds of illness. Not loving ourselves leaves us open to abusive partners, heart and lung problems and low self worth. It is so important to be good to yourself and deal with issues as they arise if possible. Bottling things up causes stress in the body and it can kill you if you allow it to persist.

22. Disease and Cell Memory

The Most of us are already aware that the human body has the ability to rejuvenate itself allowing it to self heal. The organs and cells all rejuvenate at different speeds, the eyes take approximately two days, the liver takes six weeks and we have new skin every three to four weeks. With this knowledge, you might ask the question "Why do we still have cancer in the organs if they are replaced through this rejuvenation?"

The answer is related to cell memory. The cells in the human body have a memory or blueprint that is passed on from the old cell to the new cell when it rejuvenates; each old cell passes on the exact information necessary for that cell to replicate the original even if it is diseased: thus passing on the memory of the cancer.

It is possible to break the chain by finding the initial cause of the first problem cell memory, the issue that caused the cancerous cell to turn cancerous. This could be the result of an emotional or mental trauma some time ago, for instance, a particular incident that triggered the first cell to turn cancerous.

In my experience it is possible to find out this information fairly easily by working with the inner wisdom of the human body, this is the same wisdom that keeps us breathing when we sleep and knows the function of every cell contained within it. I believe, as do many others, that we have the ability to find out that information by connecting to that inner wisdom and then working towards harmony to remove the cause of the disease. When we know what caused it, we can hopefully rectify that and cure the problem.

This wisdom can be reached via connection to the higher self as explained in the chapter "Connecting with your higher self". Finding the cause is quite often the easy bit. Next, you need to remove the memory by removing the hurtful emotions, sadness, anger, fear, etc. This can be difficult for some as they would rather not temporarily revisit the painful experience. Unfortunately it is important to sometimes go back in order to go forward and it is an important part of the healing process.

The way to access the cause is to connect with your higher self and take your conscious awareness into the tumour for example, by just setting the intention in your mind that you are inside the tumour or imagining you can see it in your minds eye. It is possible to ask your higher self or inner wisdom what caused the tumour to grow and even what will help to dissipate it, then just sit quietly and wait for the answer to come into your mind and trust the process.

Many of my clients have found the answers to why they have cancer using this technique. They then have the chance to work on releasing the particular issue or to carry out lifestyle changes necessary to heal them. This usually relates to some sort of emotional upset and the next part of the process involves working through the issues and forgiving either themselves or the other person completely.

Writing letters to the person but not sending them can help, the letters allow you to release the emotions onto the page and then you need to burn them to transmute the energy. I also occasionally take people through a meditation to discuss the issues with the other person on a soul level which can be very helpful. Once the emotional or mental issue has been released, it is necessary to work on the physical. If the tumour has not been removed by surgery, I would work on it using visualisation techniques as discussed in the chapter headed "Heal thyself" which explains the visualisation I used on my own damaged cells. The visualisation can be adapted to suit the way you see things.

Many natural remedies help with illness these days and can compliment medical treatment. Some times we will find a soul fragment as part of the healing, especially with childhood traumas, (this is explained later in the chapter about Soul Retrieval).

It is important to realise that people who hurt us are helping us to learn about life and are a necessary part of our journey and our Karma. Even though it seems unfair we should try to let go of blame as well as forgiving them and ourselves. We need to infuse love into every situation to reach the point of freedom from the stresses caused by holding on to the past. Letting go is very important and can take time. My advice is keep at it, you will get there eventually.

23. Fear

Fear is a basis survival emotion and is connected to the base chakra which is our fight or flight instinct. All forms of fear are protective instincts and should not be ignored and we need some sort of fear in order to survive. It moves us away from danger and it relates to self preservation. In a dangerous world fear should not be pandered to; however it should also not be ignored.

As you are now probably aware, like attracts like, so fearful emotions will attract fearful energies. These negative energies are attracted to fear based emotions such as anger, bitterness or rage, jealousy and vengefulness etc. We all get angry now and again and that emotion will quickly dissipate, it is being in an angry state for a long time that causes problems. This long term anger can also attract dark energies, spirits and entities to us who are attracted like a magnet to negative emotional energy.

Violence of any type is very good at attracting these very low octane energies, long term repressed negative emotions can after a while turn into a certain type of entity, these can feel dense and look like a black mass of energy, some may even have tentacles looking more like something from the abyss or from a Science Fiction movie. I removed one of these black energies the size of a car wheel, it had tentacles about 2 - 3 inches thick. It was attached to the wound of a woman I know, she was in the intensive care unit of my local hospital having contracted the killer bug that is similar to MRSA but is called necrotizing fasciitis; it literally eats your flesh away and can kill you within 24 hrs. She only went into hospital for key hole surgery to be sterilised and ended up at deaths door, she was in hospital for seven weeks all in. Thank God, she survived but has hideous scars on her body as a result of much of the dead flesh having been cut away in order to save her life

This made me think that maybe these "Bugs" so to speak are really entities that are attracted to the sick and vulnerable. The term "Entity" means a mass of invisible energy, albeit good or bad. It is not something from a horror movie, just bad energy and can easily be removed. This was not the first time I had seen and removed one of these black masses from a person in hospital. This particular lady had a brain tumour and the mass was wrapped around her head. Was it attracted to her negative thinking, did it affect the growth of the tumour or maybe it was responsible for the tumour full stop and had been there for a long period of time, who knows? I have my opinion but you need to draw your own conclusions.

Drugs and alcohol (by alcohol I mean more than one glass of wine) affect us in a negative manner. When we get drunk or "high" our crown chakra opens and we become vulnerable to all sorts of negative energies or entities and we can even become possessed. Yes, I did say possessed. Consider this for a moment, when was the last time you heard a person say "I don't know what possessed me to do that", after they have behaved out of character after one too many drinks.

These negative energies can pop into you making you take leave of your senses and exit again, leaving you to clean up their mess, or worse still they move into your body and stay, causing all sorts of problems from personality changes, alcoholism or even chronic fatigue, at the very worst, suicide. If you think this has happened to you or someone you know, you can ask permission from them do the tie cutting techniques and energy clearing, which should help. I believe it will help lots of people especially ones with health issues such as chronic fatigue by clearing the negative clouds of energy from the mental layer of the aura and clearing the crown chakra, their thinking is elevated to a higher level.

Smoking can also cause problems related to negative energies. One evening I decided to visit an old friend of mine on the way home from work. The house was full of girls getting ready for a wild night out on the town, a birthday party. They were all drinking wine and some were smoking. I had given up smoking about 18 months before but did have a cigarette now and then as I found it easy not to have a second one and just stop again. With this cigarette I also had a glass of wine. Before I left to go home, my friend gave me a hug, she was a bit worse for wear due to the wine.

The repercussions were terrible and I immediately felt what I can only describe as feeling like I had been hit in the stomach and chest with a hammer. It was a mighty bang and it left me feeling weak and sick, my heart racing I had to go straight home I felt so ill. I wondered what on earth had happened.

During that night I was awoken by alarm bells going off in my sleep. I could see in my minds eye that I had a huge 'V' shape hole in my aura. I was wide open. I soon got to work on repairing it by pulling the edges in and weaving it back together with rays of light from my finger tips. The energetic wiring in my body (meridians) had been chopped and ripped up and I felt violated to say the least.

Using visualisation techniques, I reconnected each wire and fused them back together until every wire was fixed. I did a tie cutting and could see a dark shadow around me. It must have been attached to my friend and when she hugged me it contaminated me. One cigarette had caused this problem, opening holes in my aura and allowing the shadow in. It was my own fault and I paid for that smoke severely. Smoking is not acceptable when you reach a certain level of attainment, and neither is alcohol, I know that now. It will block your spiritual growth as it is considered to be self sabotage. Sobriety is the wise choice.

The Universe will let someone or something in to sabotage you if you self sabotage, try to remember that. The higher you attain even eating the wrong foods can be considered self sabotage. If you are being attacked or sabotaged have a good look to see what you are doing to create this situation before you start to blame others.

When we are under the influence of drugs or alcohol holes open up in our aura and we have a weakened energy field as a result. When these energies get a hold we need to clear them as soon as possible and tie cutting and energy clearing can be set out with the clear intention that the disc of Crystal Ki light is to clear negative energies, emotions, entities and clear any negativity from the aura and from all levels of consciousness.

The intention is very important, for example if the issue is anger, then work on removing that, if the emotion is fear, then work on clearing that. Name the specific emotion when you set your intentions at the beginning of the tie cutting and energy clearing exercise in this book.

Simple breathing exercises can help to release fear, visualising the fear leaving on the out breath. To do this sit in a quiet place, breath in slowly on the count of five then hold your breath for five seconds, then breath out for five seconds seeing the fear leave your body in the out breath and imagine that every bit of fear is being released. Practice this over and again for at least fifteen minutes and it will help to release the fear and also aid relaxation.

24. Forgive them for you, not them!

Forgiveness is very important to our health and wellness and is a vital part of the healing process. We can be tied to someone we are in conflict with for lifetimes if we refuse to forgive them. It is not about correcting the other person for hurting you but realising that all hurt is self inflicted. We bring it all to our own door. We create our own karma and therefore we can really only trust God 100% as anyone else can let us down by delivering negative karma. Trust is naïve when you understand karma. Naïve Trust is co-dependency and this is always a problem. You can trust your husband or best friend but consider this, knowing what you do about karma and the illusion of the self created hologram we see as our 3D world.

Let's say that you trust your husband or wife 100% and you have been with them for years. Then all of a sudden they betray you and run off with someone else. Why? Karma and lessons, that's why. You may need to learn about how to handle betrayal and that is the way the Universe works. Maybe you betrayed them in a past life and your Karma has been delivered right back to you. It is important to see that they are just a part of the illusion being projected to deliver your karma in order to work off karmic debt and to see how you respond. Often it's a test and the wise choice is passive.

The whole point is to learn to forgive and accepting that the betrayal was created by your soul not the betrayer, your soul chose this experience! Your soul chooses all of your experiences in order for you to learn and grow. The person who betrayed you was just delivering your lesson or karma.

We must all learn to forgive in order to evolve and the following exercise may help you to forgive those who have hurt you in the past.

Five Steps to Forgiveness

The following exercise involves five simple steps to forgiveness and having used it myself in the past, I can recommend it as it really helped me. First find a quiet place where you will not be disturbed, you will need a pen and some paper.

Write down why you are upset or angry.
Write down the good things about the person or people who hurt you.
Write down how you contributed to the argument or problem and be honest!

Think about the law of reflection (as written in the Universal spiritual law chapter). Reflect on what you have written, looking at all three lists. Think about the person and their importance in your life. Depending on how important they are may have an effect on the relationship after you forgive them. Remember you are forgiving them for your needs and spiritual growth. The important thing is to have a good think when you are calm and the initial anger has dissipated. This may take you a little time. It does not matter; what matters is forgiveness for the sake of your peace and well being. (You can use the space clearing process in the chapter on tie cutting) to clear your anger by setting that intention). If you feel you should let go of the relationship altogether, that's fine. Tie cut and move on after you forgive them (for your sake). If you want to carry on with the relationship/friendship, great! That's also fine.

State out loud that you forgive them, you may not be able to forget but you can forgive and let go of the pain and anger. You are healing yourself by forgiving them, you are putting a stop to the negative thoughts running through your mind which if you hold on to them could damage you and can lead to serious illness as unforgiveness gets stored in the heart chakra, it can cause the heart to become diseased.

You can sit quietly and breathe out all of the anger and pain and visualize it leaving our body in the out breath. You should feel better after this; you do not even have to discuss this with the person.
If you feel you still have not quite let go enough, have a think about what is being reflected to you. What is the universe trying to show you here? Read the law of reflection in the spiritual law chapter of this book again, and then go back to step 4 and think about it a little longer. Once you are happy and feel you have forgiven them, you can burn the papers as this helps transform the energy. This may seem like a pointless exercise but it really does help, the only way to find out is to try it.

25. The Chakras and Auric Bodies

The chakra and the auric bodies are the energetic systems of a human being. Chakras are cone shaped vortexes of light shaped like a small tornado with the point of the cone connecting to the main channel which runs down the spine from the crown to the base. These energy centres are spinning wheels of light and vary in colour depending upon their frequency and position. They directly relate to mental, emotional, physical and spiritual health. There are hundreds of other smaller chakras each connected to an acupressure or an acupuncture point. These energy centres are interconnected, working in unison and in balancing one, you will affect the others.

Most books relate to 7 chakras but I tend to work on 12, 10 in the body and 1 above the head (higher crown) and 1 below the feet (earth star chakra). The 8 main chakras radiate out from the main channel running down the spinal column forming the vertical axis. The chakras are what keep us alive and keep us in our physical form, without them we would not be here; it is therefore vital that we care for these energy centres. As we raise our vibration we cleanse and clear these chakras, we wake up to a higher level of awareness as a result, especially when we balance the crown chakra and learn to connect to our higher selves.

A healthy chakra will be brightly coloured and spinning clockwise whereas an unhealthy chakra will be dull and if it is trying to clear itself, it will be spinning counter clockwise. These energy centres respond to all forms of stimuli and pass on the messages they receive to the internal organs and the physical body as a whole. They affect everything and can become unbalanced by our lifestyle, mental attitude, our sexual behaviour, emotional and physical activities. Even the colour of the food we eat can affect the chakras. That is why it is good to have many colours of food on your plate and to eat plenty of greens as green is the colour of the heart chakra.

Problems can begin way out in the auric bodies and filter down through the layers and can eventually cause disease in the physical body. The aura is a bio-energetic sheath covering the whole physical body and is made up of many different layers of which we will discuss 7; however there are many other layers.

During the last 2500 years of the Piscean Age people have primarily been working on one body or at the most two or three bodies. We now need to cleanse and develop all of these bodies to achieve the necessary unity for utilizing the power of Aquarian Age energies. One aspect of the Aquarian Age is increased awareness of the physical body and its functions. Most of us have been trained to rely primarily on our brainpower for information, but by tuning into the consciousness received through the body by the chakras, we will become more in tune with higher mental and spiritual energies and free from restrictions and brain programming. Development and use of the brain was very important in the Piscean Age, but now we also need to expand to higher octaves of mental and spiritual energies.

All healing and ascension processes are working towards integrating our spiritual light body into our lower physical body. We bring the new energies down to us and anchor them into our energetic bodies; it is not us going up to them, as the word ascension suggests.

In order to fully integrate your light body (Merkaba) you will need to reactivate your dormant DNA. It is possible to reactivate your twelve strand DNA by visiting a practitioner who knows how to do it or through prayer and meditation. Simply set your intention to connect with God, the first creator and ask him to begin to reactivate your full twelve strands of DNA, NOW! Then use the tie cutting techniques to remove any implants that may be blocking the DNA functioning. Full activation can be achieved in as little as three months.

Prayer can also be used to remove implants. These are etheric implants placed in us to stop DNA function. We should open our minds safely to higher level of consciousness and not too quickly as it can literally blow your mind and damage your nervous system. A simple prayer to God, the first creator asking him to remove all implants, NOW! Make sure that you say now with meaning. Then brace yourself as the energy can shift very quickly through your body.

It is also possible to release the death hormone and reprogram the rejuvenation hormone but I am not at liberty to give you that information in this book. You may be given this information through meditation when you are ready and not before.

The purpose of this healing is to clear your endocrine and hormonal systems, allowing your light body to be aligned throughout your chakra system allowing for ascension by the process of raising your vibration. I use grids of light to cleanse the chakras and reprogram the cell memory and it works well, others use mantras and meditation. These changes affect the endocrine system and the hormonal system. The endocrine system monitors everything within the physical body it monitors and adjusts everything regulating your organs at a cellular level keeping the functioning correct. It also has a primary function of connecting the lower physical energies to the higher spiritual energies. Once these changes take place, more energy can flow via the DNA strands, the chakras, the endocrine and the hormonal systems. As they are restored to their primary purpose we are fully able to recognise the Christ consciousness within each and every one of us.

This may all sound very complicated, but the subconscious can be reprogrammed in a matter of minutes and I do it at the end of treatments with my clients who are at the correct level of consciousness and are ready for the process to be carried out. It can transform their lives by removing negative patterns on a deep subconscious level.

The Auric Bodies (Bioenergetic sheath)
Physical Body
The physical body is the densest of the seven bodies, the only one which can be seen without clairvoyant vision. With the physical body, we express, we receive, and we become aware.

Emotional Body
The emotional body has a vibratory rate through which we feel and express emotions; it is also a passageway to the divine when fully developed serves as an outlet for feelings of divine love.

Mental Body
The mental body is the vibratory rate through which we think and reason. When we operate in the lower levels of the mental body, our thoughts and attitudes may be heavily influenced by feelings, giving rise to "desire mind", products of which include prejudices, opinions and other forms of emotional thinking. Operating at higher levels of the mental body we are

capable of abstract thinking, creativity, logical reasoning, mathematics and philosophy.

Intuitional/Compassionate Body

This is a vibratory rate where one feels compassion and has understanding of self and others. It is also a vehicle for the expression of higher forms of love, a gateway to the Divine, serving as a connecting link between the emotional and the divine levels. In this body, we are above the limits of time and space; there is understanding without the need to go through a process of reasoning and thinking. This is the home of intuition.

Will/Spirit Body

The Will/Spirit body is the vehicle or vibratory rate through which spirit expresses. It channels energy which manifests as will and is said to be the highest level a person can reach and still negate the Divine or Soul levels; this brings a possibility of great negativity or karma because the energy is so high. This is the area for choice, Divine will, or the individual will.

Soul Body

The soul body is the vehicle for the expression of soul energies, where one experiences self as one with God, self experienced as a unit of God's consciousness.

Divine Body

The Divine body is the seventh. In this body we relate to the spark of the divine within us. We can deeply feel the presence of God in our lives and feel oneness with a divine reality.

Chakras and Colours

Chakra colours mean various things and new colours are coming through from the Universe and are much more opalescent in appearance. They include a pinkie-orange, a lime green, a petrol blue, a deep royal purple, aquamarine and a deep dark pink. I have listed the original colours below.

Red – Passion, life energy
Orange – Creativity and feminine energy
Yellow – Wisdom and power and intellect
Green / Pink – Healing and Love
Aquamarine – Unconditional love
Turquoise blue – Communication
Indigo blue – Intuition and guidance
Purple / White– Vision and spirituality
Silver – The transference of energy and a clear human connection to the divine
Gold - Soul purpose and harmony
Pearl White – Source Energy

THE 12 CHAKRAS

The Stellar Gateway
Gold - This is depicted as a tunnel of pure light or a portal that connects the soul to the Divine Source. Activation and clearing of this chakra opens a cosmic doorway to all of the Light Densities and enhances communication with Enlightened Beings that exist in the Densities of Light beyond the physical worlds. Its purpose is to maintain a link between the creator and creation. It is through this chakra that highly spiritual humans will experience ultimate consciousness. Accessing this centre can be detrimental to the mental health unless the person is ready and spiritually evolved.

Soul Star (Higher Crown Chakra)
White - It is through this chakra that the soul braids into the physical at the time of incarnation (Birth) and it is through this chakra the soul leaves the physical body when we die. Access to the soul star chakra

increases direct contact with the soul and the communication of the soul's intent is enhanced.

The Causal Chakra
Silver - This important Vortex lies at the outer edge of the aura and regulates the flow of energy from the Soul Star Chakra to the body. In practice, it regulates Soul-braiding and enables the physical body to attune to the increased energy of Soul Consciousness and to the Higher Density Light existence resulting from the Soul-braiding. The causal chakra is the centre that accepts the "dosages" of light that the upper two chakras deliver, and it assists in higher activations of the crown, brow and throat chakras.

Crown Chakra
Violet – Associated with enlightenment, meanings of life and existence. Shimmering golden white – Associated with the state of perfection in mind body, emotions and spirituality. It is the most purely spiritual chakra. It is through this centre we gain wisdom from the spirit realm and the connection to cosmic consciousness. When clear we are able to see through the illusion, we become self aware and can consciously detach from personal emotions. It vitalises the cerebrum, right eye and the pineal gland. Once activated you begin to realise "who you are". It governs the upper brain and the pineal gland. It facilitates connection to the higher self, inner guidance, the higher levels of consciousness, oneness, unconditional love, spiritual awareness, intuition and wisdom. It is the main entry point for our incarnation and life force. When blocked we feel weak and low.

Brow Chakra (Third Eye)
Indigo – Associated with attainment, the pursuit for our spiritual purpose in life. It is located above the eye brows in the middle of the forehead. It is the centre of

psychic power, psychic vision, higher intuition, spiritual energies, magnetic forces and light. When activated one's perception of life will alter for the better. It allows access to higher information via intuition and the connection to outside guidance. It helps us to release negative tendencies and selfish attitudes. It governs the lower left brain, left eye, nose, ears, spine, pituitary gland, face, central nervous system and the production of hormones. It is the centre of will, inner vision, thought control, inspiration, clairvoyance and spiritual awakening. This chakra is interconnected to the sacral chakra.

Throat Chakra
Blue – Associated with knowledge of the Oneness with Divine guidance, located at the centre of the throat. We are able to look at multiple perspectives when this centre is activated. It is the centre of communication, sound and expression of creativity via thought, speech and writing. It is the centre of openness and the ability to hear other peoples' opinions and points of view, creativity, judgement, self expression and a sense of responsibility. It governs the throat, thyroid, four Para-thyroids, bronchial, oesophagus, vocal chords, neck, arms, digestive tract, lungs, jaws and cheeks. This centre vitalises the breath and the body's metabolic rate.

Thymus chakra/Higher Heart Chakra
This chakra represents our protection of ourselves; the associated colour is blue/green (Aquamarine). It is the filter between the head and the heart. It is located between the throat and the heart, linked to the immune system. An imbalance here can show itself as HIV/aids, auto immune disorders and recurrent viral/bactericidal illness, glandular fever, lymphatic blockages, repeated colds and coughs that can be difficult to shake off. It governs loving communication and when balanced, you may notice that you are not

allowing negative people to effect you so much, you are not catching every virus that comes along and your emotions are felt deeply and released quickly. Where the heart chakra radiates human love, the thymus chakra or higher heart as it is also referred to radiates unconditional love and the Christ/Buddha consciousness.

Heart Chakra
Pink – Associated with softness, compassion, empathy and pure emotions such as love. The primary function of the heart chakra is to link the higher levels of consciousness to the physical; it is the astral bridge. Its secondary function is the expression of love of self and others.

Green – Associated with healing, ecstasy and exhilaration. It is located in the centre of the chest. This is the centre of love, spirituality and with the "Oneness" of the Universe, compassion and group consciousness. It vitalises the heart, lungs, thymus, blood system, cellular structure, skin and hands. It is the emotional centre, sympathy, spiritual development, selflessness, forgiveness, devotion, trust, peace and healing. Most healers work through their heart chakras and if you find a good one, their higher heart. You can feel the difference when you are with someone who has their higher heart chakra functioning. They radiate a beautiful energy which is very uplifting and peaceful.

Solar Plexus
Yellow – Associated with meditative, analytical thought and intellectual activity. It is located below the breast bone. This centre is the store of Ki (Universal life force) and personal power, ambition, intellect, strength, fear, jealousy, loss of love, tolerance, wisdom, inner calm, peace, and acceptance of others. It vitalises the stomach, liver, gall bladder, spleen,

large and small intestines, sympathetic nervous system, pancreas and adrenal glands. Each of the organs in the body deals with a certain emotion. E.g. liver – jealousy and fear, kidneys – fear, spleen – anger.

Sacral Chakra
Orange – Associated with wisdom, creativity and benevolence to all. It is located approximately two inches below the navel at the pelvis just below the junction with the spine. Lots of people get pain in the lower back due to old repressed emotions. A good cry will help release the tension in this area. It is the centre that governs the digestive system and the reproductive organs. It is attuned to the emotions and thoughts concerning wellness. It is linked to the brow chakra and when balanced it assists in the development of psychic skills. It is the zone of vitality, enjoyment, self esteem, awe, sensuality, eroticism, enthusiasm and relationships. Its primary function is creativity. Its secondary function is sexual relationships and sexual activity. The latter remaining dormant until puberty which then stimulates the onset of hormonal changes in the body. It is linked with the brow chakra.

Base Chakra (Root Chakra)
Black – Associated with stability and grounding to the source of security located at the base of the spine. Black has all of the colours of the rainbow in it and should not be feared. Black crystals are very grounding.

Red – Associated with the essential, idealistic and confident passion for life. It is linked to kundalini, psychic potential, adrenal glands, teeth, nails, anus, legs, kidneys, urinary system, skin, muscles, blood, intestines, prostate gland, bladder, bones and skeletal structure. It is the centre of vitality, physical energy and self preservation. It is the zone of fight or flight. Many people have an imbalance here because the fight or flight response is not allowed to be acted upon. Fighting is socially unacceptable and so is running away.

Knee Chakras
The knee chakras are minor chakras governing movement and the gateway for grounding the soul into form. The associated colour is maroon. Most knee problems are a result of the energy becoming turned off from the knee down to the feet. Working on the knees allows the energy to flow freely down to the feet and earth star chakra. It governs strength of purpose, our worthiness as well as the shoulder and neck muscles. It also monitors the flow of the body's energies.

Feet Chakras
The feet Chakras govern balance, wholeness and the logic mind. They regulate the flow of the body's energy from the physical layer to the spiritual layer. The feet chakras are minor chakras but none the less important regarding our connection to earth and grounding the body's energy. The associated colour is brown. Placing your hands on the client's shoulders causes the feet chakras to open and thus helps to ground them. Grounding is essential to both the healer and the client.

The Earth Star Chakra
This is located between and slightly below the feet (approx' 12 inches). It links the physical body to the earth via a vibratory energetic cord that hooks into the earth and holds the etheric bodies and the soul incarnate. It governs bonding and produces a sense of connectedness and a sense of community. The associated colour is dark brown.

THE CHAKRAS

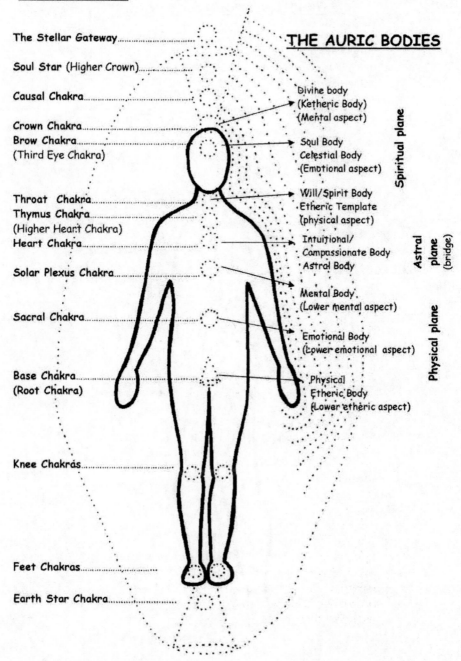

The Stellar Gateway.................

Soul Star (Higher Crown)............

Causal Chakra.................

Crown Chakra..............
Brow Chakra.............
(Third Eye Chakra)

Throat Chakra.............
Thymus Chakra............
(Higher Heart Chakra)
Heart Chakra...........

Solar Plexus Chakra.............

Sacral Chakra...........

Base Chakra..........
(Root Chakra)

Knee Chakras..............

Feet Chakras.............

Earth Star Chakra............

THE AURIC BODIES

Divine body
(Ketheric Body)
(Mental aspect)

Soul Body
Celestial Body
(Emotional aspect)

Will/Spirit Body
Etheric Template
(physical aspect)

Intuitional/
Compassionate Body
Astral Body

Mental Body
(Lower mental aspect)

Emotional Body
(Lower emotional aspect)

Physical
Etheric Body
(Lower etheric aspect)

Spiritual plane

Astral plane (bridge)

Physical plane

Diagram 1 - Adapted from Barbara Ann Brennan's - Hands of Light

Main Chakras (Side View)

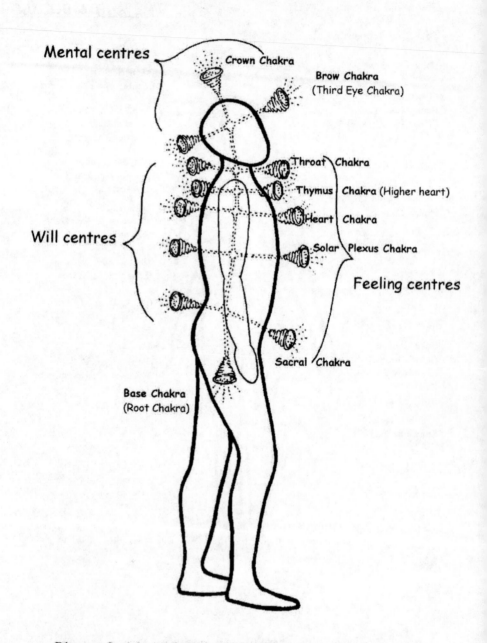

Mental centres

Crown Chakra

Brow Chakra
(Third Eye Chakra)

Throat Chakra

Thymus Chakra (Higher heart)

Heart Chakra

Solar Plexus Chakra

Will centres

Feeling centres

Sacral Chakra

Base Chakra
(Root Chakra)

Diagram 2 - Adapted from Barbara Ann Brennan's - Hands of Light

26. Connecting to your Higher Self

Another useful exercise is learning how to connect to your higher self, you can find out all sorts of useful information from a higher level of consciousness. Some people find it hard to visualise or they think that they need to have amazing visual pictures in their minds eye; this is not the case. If you find it difficult to visualise, try to imagine it in your minds eye instead or sense it with your feelings. It will work just as well as visualising.

The two simple ways to do this are as follows....

1. Visualise a golden orb of light representing your higher self and resting about 30cm (12 inches) above your head. Then see a line of light coming down in through your crown chakra on the top of your head and entering your conscious mind. I see it as a kind of cosmic telephone cable.

2. You can also visualise your Christ-self or your Buddha-self, and see that image floating down from above your head and coming into your mind setting the intention that you are connected to your higher self. Once you are connected begin with the following breathing exercises which will take your brain waves to a more medative state.

Close your eyes and take 6 long, slow deep breaths in through your nose and filling your whole body with air, allowing your chest and stomach to rise and right down into your abdomen then slowly breathe out through your mouth. (With each of the 6 breaths feel yourself relaxing more and more and visualise any stress leaving your body in the out breath).

Take 6 slow breaths into your lungs only, expanding the chest, breathing in through the nose and out through the mouth.

Take 6 slow breaths into the upper chest only once again in through the nose and out through the mouth.

Allow your breath to find its own natural rhythm and just relax for a couple of minutes.

Relax and let the information you need come into your mind and feel the peace flow through your whole body.

When you are finished, drink some water to ground yourself. (You might like to set an alarm for 10 – 15 minutes in case you fall asleep).

Once you are in this semi medative state a lot of information can come in very quickly, and so you can begin to ask questions, and the first thing that comes to mind is the answer. I do this with my clients and students a lot, and they often ask me how do I know it's my higher self and not my ego or imagination? Well I always say the fact that you have gone through the process of clearing and entering a meditative state creating the change in brainwaves will more or less guarantee that the information is coming from your higher self.

Being connected to your higher self is an amazing and powerful tool. You can also use this process to help you become more creative. Let's say for example you wanted to paint a picture, write an essay or decorate a room. Before you go to bed just ask your higher self to work on those ideas and to create the images you need whilst you sleep. Let your higher self do some of the work. The next day when you connect with your higher self you can get all of the ideas that came in the night and then put those ideas into practice.

I connect to a higher level of consciousness when I work with my clients, as I like my information to come from my higher consciousness and not my ego self. I do this before I start a treatment or when doing journey work or any healing work on myself. I know then that any information coming to me is from a higher source, a much wiser source, and this has helped me to grow in confidence so much over the years, being able to make this conscious connection.

The other thing to do when working with your higher mind is to ensure that you are grounded. I do this by visualising an orb of light (1m (3ft) in diameter) around my earth star chakra which is about 30cm (12 inches) beneath my feet below the ground. I visualise an orb of energy which I then camouflage and seeing a connection from the base of my spine going down my legs and out to my feet and connecting to the earth star chakra inside that protective orb. I state that this orb is to act as a filter to purify any negative energies coming into my body from the ground. I have seen lots of lower octave energy in the ground that is not for the highest good and my guidance was to protect myself from it and this technique works very well for me.

It is very important to do this otherwise during meditation and working with the higher mind, you are likely to feel other worldly, spaced out, and light headed, so it is important to ground yourself. Drinking water will also help you to ground or stamping your feet firmly on the floor can also help.

I would recommend an energy clearing before you start to ensure that the information is from your higher self and not any other source. Spirits or other energies can interfere with guidance and they are not always easy to sense. Some of the negative energies out there can actually hook into people and drain their energy or manipulate them via a kind of lease or chain; even people who surround themselves in white light are vulnerable.

It is important to be discerning as just because something tells you it is an angel, does not mean that it really is. Personally I believe surrounding yourself in white light attracts moths and it is safer to ask your higher self to choose the energy that you need to protect you. A tie cutting and space clearing will remove these unwanted energies.

27. Tie Cutting and Energy Clearing

Of all of the information and meditations exercises I have learned over the years these tie cutting and energy clearing techniques have served the most useful and powerful, so much so, that they are part of my daily routine. I have seen many good healers and therapists go wayside as a result of negative attachments that have hooked into their weaker ego self and these things are very subtle. Luckily, I can sense them almost immediately and they have trouble sticking to me. It has made me quite sad at times but they are learning valuable lessons from these things as we all are on some level.

Very early on in my awakening, I realised that I needed to be free from other peoples negative connections to me in order to get to where I was meant to be even though at the time I was not really sure where I was going spiritually. But this information has been vital and has helped me to reach my enlightened state of being and I am eternally grateful to Archangel Michael for teaching me the clearing techniques. He feels more like my elder brother than a celestial being and I always feel safe because of his presence.

The Tie cutting and energy clearing I teach in my workshops can be used to clear your energy field, the energy in your home or work place and so on. You can use it on friends and family even pets and plants. It can be used at a distant even if they are in Australia, it will still work as well as if they were in the same room. You must get permission first, always! If not you may suffer the consequences of your pushy uninvited actions, so I would advise you to use it wisely. All energy work must be carried out with care and attention to detail.

I will explain how the procedure is carried out first, and then give you the information in the form of an exercise to use on yourself. I will explain distant clearing and as you become more familiar with the exercise you can work on distant cleansings. The more you use it on yourself the quicker you will be able to perform the cleansing. I recommend practising it at least once a day for 21 days, at the end of the 21 days; you will know it by heart and can use it anywhere. It comes in handy and I even use it to clear hotel rooms when I am on holiday or at workshops, I like to sleep in a clear space.

The first thing to do is to say a brief prayer before you start asking God to guide and protect you and your work to ensure that all energies that come to you, come from God. I never work without starting with a prayer, it is very important. I then invoke the Crystal Ki energies to work with me and set my intention meaning what you intend to happen and the goal of this exercise.

When performing an energy clearing on yourself. You can do it sitting in a chair. I work right out into my aura to level 35 which I feel is just outside of my God Self layer of my aura which is layer 33. (It is possible to take a lift in meditation to level 33 and converse directly with God if you so wish, I do it often). Once I have asked the energies to cut and release the negativity, I see the disc or grid of light moving down through all of the levels in my aura, 35, 30, 25, 20, 15, 10, 5, into the crown chakra on top of my head, then slowly down through my physical body and out of the soles of my feet and down through the aura below me to level 35. That way I have cleared a sphere of my aura that is just outside of my God self layer. As a beginner you might like to start at level 5 and come down 5, 4, 3, 2, 1, and into your body, bring the grid slowly down through your whole body, out of your feet and down into the aura below you, 1, 2, 3, 4, 5 levels. You can think of these levels in terms of metres if it helps your visualisation. The intention is the most important thing; the Crystal Ki energies will do the rest. As you feel more confident, you can increase the levels from 5 to 10, then 20 until you feel happy to work on 35 levels.

Once you have brought the grid through your energy field, you can then ask the Universal Crystal Ki energies of purification to collect the debris and take it to where God wills it to be, which is either into the light, into the central flame or back to where it came from whichever is Gods Will. If you have worked on the first 5 layers or metres, try to visualise a net ball of light forming from the lowest point 5m below you, moving up and around the sides of the 5m radius sphere and over the top of your aura to 5m above you. I like to see it tied at the top so as not to let any thing leak out. Your aura is now encased in a net ball of light which will remove the debris cut free by the grid of light.

Now ask the Crystal Ki energies to remove the net and see the bottom of the ball moving up through the aura from 5, 4, 3, 2, 1, and into your feet, then slowly up through your body and out of the top of your head. Then continue up through your aura again, from 1, 2, 3, 4, 5. At this point have a look in your minds eye to see what is in the net and then see it disappear into the distance as the Crystal Ki energies take it to where God wills it to be.

Sometimes the net may be too heavy to lift or have liquid in it. If this is the case, just ask for the net to be either water tight or to be reinforced to make it stronger and ask the energies to bring the net ball around you, then through you and your aura again. Never panic as the Crystal Ki energies are there to help and all you need to do is ask for guidance and you will receive it.

You are now clear of the rubbish and you need to ask God and the Crystal Ki energies to fill the voids with whatever is necessary. THIS IS IMPORTANT! If you do not do this, you leave yourself wide open to be filled with more rubbish. You can do this clearing on your house if you are sitting inside of it using the same procedure but setting the intention to clear the house instead of yourself.

Distant Clearing

This involves the same technique except that you visualise the person standing about 50m away from you and see them as transparent in order to see the grid of light move through them easily. See the grid moving down through their aura and through them and out of the bottom of their feet into the aura below them. Visualise the net ball of light forming from below them and around the sides of their aura and over the top of them until they are also surrounded in a sphere of light. Visualise the ball moving up through their aura, their physical body and the aura above them and see it being taken away by the Crystal Ki energies.

Ask God and the energies to fill the voids with exactly what they need and wait a couple of minutes for this to happen and the clearing is complete. This procedure is very powerful and can be done on people, animals, countries and even Mother Earth if you care to try. I regularly clear the planet using this technique but could do with more like minds to learn the procedure as working at this level takes a lot of energy. I find that I lose weight when I do a lot of planetary healing.

To do this distant clearing on a building, the same procedure applies. Visualise the building as a simple glass box; this box represents the building you wish to cleanse. See the grid coming down from about 10m above the roof and down through the building, through each floor and then down into the ground about 10m below ground level will do. Then just as you would with a person, see the net ball of light surround the building and see it rising up from below the ground through the building and up into air 10m. I like to look at this point to make sure that there is something in the net before asking the Crystal Ki energies to take it to where God wills it to be. Then ask them to fill the voids and allow this to happen. It really is quite simple and practise is essential if you want your home or work place to be clear.

If you have a problem seeing the net in your minds eye, just imagine that it is happening, this is good enough but just saying the words and not visualising it is pointless and it will not work. It is important that you are not going to be disturbed as once you have started the procedure, you must see it through to completion as not doing so can be counter productive.

Tie Cutting

Tie cutting is simple and can release us from unhealthy or controlling relationships, past traumas and much more. I have even used it to cut ties with my self saboteur and asking the Universe to bring in the improved version of me, visualising that new me coming all of the way into my physical body and merging with my energy. I'm sure this helped me to get motivated and to write this book.

Most of you will have heard the old saying "Tugging at my heart strings". These strings are real albeit invisible to the naked eye. They are negative energetic psychic ties or connections. Tie cutting literally cuts you free of these connections and freedom prevails. Not being able to move on from old lovers is the most common problem tie cutting resolves but many people need to cut ties with their own family as they can cause us a lot of distress. People can drain your life force via these connections, leaving you feeling depleted when they have gone. It is simple to cut them using this visualisation technique having first set the intention that you wish to cut the negative tie between you and whom ever you choose.

1. First find a quiet place where you will not be disturbed and set your intention to cut only the negative ties with this person or group.

2. Do the 18 breath exercise to help open your minds eye.

3. Visualise that person standing about 10m away from you and try to get a sense of the negative

connection or tie. If you cannot see one don't worry, simply imagine a black ribbon connecting you both.

4. In your minds eye visualise a pair of scissors cutting that ribbon and then say these words and mean them, "I cut and release you with love and peace, I am totally free". This will release the energy you have cut free. I have seen ropes, rods, chains and other things linking people together. Depending on what needs cutting, you can visualise either using a knife, bolt cutters for chains or a laser for metal rods. Just visualising the tool coming in and cutting the negative tie will do the job.

5. Ask God to fill the gaps with whatever is necessary at this time and say thank you.

This can also be used to cut free earthbound spirits. I once had a client who had the spirit of her brother attached to her, He had died when they were children and she was now in her fifties. During the Crystal Ki chakra balancing treatment, her deceased brother told me that he wanted her to carry out a tie cutting in order for him to pass over into the light. This is always a difficult position for me but I did tell the lady and she was very grateful. I took her into a meditative state and let her talk to her brother and say goodbye, it was very moving for all of us. It was the right thing to do though and the lady was pleased that he was ok and that she had the chance to say goodbye to him. I love my work but sometimes it can get very emotional.

Note: Negative ties made with people due to fall outs and disputes can be reconnected if you still persist in arguing or bad mouthing the person you have cut ties with. So I advise you to cut, release and forgive once and for all. These connections can drain your energy and it is only yourself that you are hurting in the end.

The most important thing is to set your intention, and not to do this to anyone without their permission although it is alright to do it to children without theirs as they are not old enough to make the decision for themselves. However if you are performing this on someone, and you are unable to seek their permission you can always ask their higher self and the best way to do this is to ask your higher self to ask theirs higher self for permission and to question if the tie cutting and energy clearing is for their highest good. If the response is anything other than a definite yes, then do not perform any tie cutting or any energy clearing, as you could be disrupting their karma and that is not allowed. It is possible that the Universe is trying to teach them a lesson and we should keep away and let nature take its course.

The same is true with someone's property, unless you have been given permission from the person who owns the property; you do not have any rights to do an energy clearing on it even if you detect any negative energy in there. You are allowed to clear the building you work in, but it is important to do it when the building is as empty as possible, and set the intention that you aim to clear any negative energy only contained within the building and not the people possibly still in there.

Space clearing on a person exercise

1. Prayer....Dear God, I ask that I am a channel of pure love and light, that all energies and information that comes to me, comes from you. I ask that this healing is for the highest good of all. Please bless and protect me as I work. Amen.

2. Affirm...I call upon the Universal Crystal Ki Healing Energies and the Energies of Purification. (3 Times)

3. Affirm....My intention is to cut and release only negative ties, to cut and release, record, memory, cause and effect all negative psychic ties, cords, chains, implants, symbols and connections on all levels not for the highest good of all, to be free from all those incarnate and discarnate, all negative energies, ET's or entities, to be free from individuals, parallel dimensions, groups, places, events, countries, to be free from the effects of lifetimes. To be set free, free to be.

4. Take 18 slow breaths starting with 6 in through the nose and filling your whole body right down into the abdomen, and then breathe out through the mouth. Take 6 breaths in through the nose, filling the lungs and rib cage only, breathe out through the mouth. Then 6 breaths in through the nose just filling the upper chest this time and out through the mouth. Then allow your breath to find its own natural rhythm. This breathing technique stimulates the pineal gland and opens the minds eye. It also helps you to relax.

5. Affirm.... I ask the Crystal Ki Energies to cut and release all negativity as stated in my earlier intentions. If this be Gods will, so be it and so it is.

6. Close your eyes, wait a minute and visualise the cutting taking place.......Visualise a 5 metre radius grid or disc of light moving down from 5m above your head through your aura and physical body, then out of the soles of your feet through your aura again to 5m below you. (You may feel a little lighter after the ties have been cut.)

7. Affirm.... I ask the Crystal Ki Energies of Purification to net, release, record, memory, cause and effect and take all negativity and debris cut free to be transformed and transmuted in the Central Flame,

taken into the Light or be returned to where it came from, whichever is Gods will.

8. Close your eyes and wait a minute visualising the netting and releasing taking place.
Visualise a net ball of light forming, starting 5m below you and surrounding the 5m radius sphere of your body's aura and tied at the top. You and your aura are now surrounded in a net ball made of light. Visualise the bottom of the ball moving upwards through the bottom of your aura, then slowly through your physical body and up into the air 5m collecting all of the rubbish that has been cut free. Have a look with your minds eye to see what is in it. Do not worry if you can not see anything, the tie cutting will still work. Then visualise the rubbish being taken away to where God wills it to be as set in the intention made earlier.
(You may feel the energy change after this.)

9. Affirm.... I ask God and the Crystal Ki Energies to please fill the voids with whatever is Gods Will. This is very important! (Wait a minute or two while this takes place).

10. I ask my higher self to choose the protection I may need at this moment in time and wait 10 or 20 seconds for that to settle in.

Thank God and the Crystal Ki Energies for helping you!!!
Dismiss the angels with love and peace.

It is essential that you carry out this exercise as it is written and I advise you to use it with the utmost integrity, it is very powerful!
(If you are any doubt about using it, please contact me via info@crystalki.co.uk for more information).

This technique can be used to remove all sorts of things such as toxins, negative belief patterns and even the seed fear of enlightenment. The seed fear of enlightenment is a kind of etheric implant that we have placed in ourselves to block us from reaching the enlightenment level of consciousness. It relates back to when we were in Atlantis. We knew then that when we became enlightened we would in effect die and this is where the fear comes from. This fear can be removed easily and we now know that enlightenment does not mean sudden death as there are many enlightened beings walking the planet and hopefully there will be many more as we all work towards ascension.

I removed my seed fear as I found out it had been placed in me by myself in my previous life having attained to the level of 904 on Dr Hawkins map of consciousness; I became fearful of death and placed the block in my body as a result. The block looked like a huge sheet of steel like a drain cover splitting my body in two halves. It came out easily in the net but you need to set the intention that you wish to remove the seed fear of enlightenment before you begin the procedure. I feel much closer to Source since I removed it.

Intention is important:
Intention is the power behind the cleansing and in fact all healing work. You are, with the help of the Universal Crystal Ki energies changing etheric energy into spiritual energy when you condition it with spiritual intent. As a result, this energy will channel through your heart chakra and raise the frequency of the energy promoting a more positive result when performing healing, distant healing global healing or enhancing meditation.

I never carry out any type of healing work without first setting clear intentions and I would strongly advise you to do the same. These energies must be treated with respect. The intention makes the work happen in the correct manner. It is best to do this exercise when you are wide awake as falling asleep half way through would leave you wide open to all sorts of rubbish in the atmosphere. I would also advise you to never work with energy when you have drugs or alcohol in your system as it can be very dangerous.

28. Meditation and Brainwaves

Meditation is practised by many different people for many different reasons. Some are religious, some spiritual, and some just for relaxation or stress management. It is very helpful in allowing you to go within and helping you to forget about the worries of the world outside.

I would highly recommend that you try to meditate on a daily basis even if only for 5-10 minutes. It is a vital tool in order to ascend to higher realms of spirituality and to access knowledge from a higher source. Meditation takes you into another state of consciousness and changes your brainwave frequency. There are 4 main states we can be in at any one time. Alpha, Beta, Delta and Theta, each having a different frequency measured in HZ (Hertz – cycles per second).

The dream state or very relaxed state is call the Alpha and its frequency varies from approx' 8-13Hz. The normal active daily waking state is called the Beta state and is around 14-30Hz. When you are day dreaming, meditating, shamanic journeying or similar, you are in the Theta state which is between 4-7Hz approx'. You are actually in this state when you are driving on the motorway and you can't remember the last few minutes of your journey. Scary stuff! The last state is Delta, this is usually reached when you are in a deep sleep, usually around 3Hz or less.

I regularly practise meditation for spiritual reasons. I use it to connect to my higher self or Source seeking divine wisdom. It is essential to my spiritual growth and has become a major part of my life. I certainly feel it if I miss my practise for a couple of days. 20 minutes a day in deep meditation is usually all I need to find the answers to any problem I encounter. But I tend to meditate in my bath for an hour at a time. It also leaves me feeling very calm and relaxed and mentally problem free.

Problems are all relative to perception and perception is illusory. These negative perceptions begin within the mind and in order to eliminate the problem we need to ask God or Source to raise the frequency of our minds and hence our perceptions. Infusing spiritual energy into the problem or situation raises the vibration and purifies the energy which means that the problem is now in a higher frequency range or has even been resolved instantaneously due to your higher consciousness and the change in your perception.

For example: A while ago, I had arrived at Birmingham airport after an 8 hour over night flight, I was exhausted as I did not sleep and I had ordered a taxi to be waiting for me when I arrived, so as to get home as soon as possible. Needless to say, the cab did not turn up. I was angry at first but then remembered that I could change my reality by asking for Divine help. I asked God to help me get home and two minutes later a taxi driver who was waiting for his pre-booked fare came over to me and asked me if I was going to Warwick University. I said no but I wanted to get home to Warwick and my cab had let me down. His fare had let him down also, so we were the answer to both of our problems. My solution had come immediately I asked God to help. It really does work, just believe and give it a try.

Practising meditation helps to clear the mind of problems and clutter and it is fairly easy to learn. The following breathing technique can be used to reach the Theta state of brainwaves. It stimulates the pineal gland opening the astral doorway to other levels of consciousness and dimensions. I also use it to bring my clients into a semi-meditative state and to help them to relax at the beginning of a session. You will need to find a quiet place where you will not be disturbed if you want to practise meditation. I always visualise a protective sphere of light around me and state that I am safe and protected by the Universe before I begin.

Sit with your back straight or lie down with a small pillow under your head. Set an alarm clock for 10-20 minutes in case you fall asleep. Before you start, you can set a subject for your meditation to be based on or ask a question of your higher self or Source.

Close your eyes and take 6 long, slow deep breaths in through your nose and filling your whole body with air, allowing your chest and stomach to rise and right down into your abdomen then slowly breathe out through your mouth. (With each of the 6 breaths feel yourself relaxing more and more and visualise any stress leaving your body in the out breath).

Take 6 slow breaths into your lungs only, expanding the chest, breathing in through the nose and out through the mouth.

Take 6 slow breaths into the upper chest only once again in through the nose and out through the mouth.

Allow your breath to find its own natural rhythm and just relax for a couple of minutes.

Relax and let the information you need come into your mind and feel the peace flow through your whole body.
When your alarm goes off, slowly bring your attention back into room and drink some water to ground yourself.

If you still feel a bit light headed; visualise a sphere of light around your earth star chakra. This is situated approx' 30cm (12 inches) below the soles of you feet – see diagram 1). See the outside of the sphere as camouflaged if you feel the need, I always do to keep the moths away: sometimes it is sensible to hide your light when you are in certain places as lower frequency energies will not be able to see you as easily. Set the intention that the sphere is to act as a protective filter and to purify any energy coming into your body via the chakras on the soles of your feet.

Then take your attention to the top of your head (Crown chakra) and visualise a line of light moving down from your crown, through your main channel along the front of the spine, down your legs and out of your feet into your earth star chakra inside the sphere. You have grounded your energy by doing this.

There are many types of meditation techniques....

Mindfulness meditation – Open focus, remaining in the here and now. Shifting from one thought to the next with ease and complete acceptance of all things. The person constantly brings the mind back to the now and does not analyse or fantasise in any way.

Concentrated meditation – this is about being focused on an object or repeating a mantra or prayer.

Buddhist Meditation – this includes shamantha which is focused on a single subject and vipassana which is aimed at developing wisdom and insight through seeing the truth.

There are many other types of meditation and I advise you to read about a few before choosing one. Some methods involve keeping the eyes open and staring at a particular point or object. I found this difficult and it made my eyes water. When I meditate, I ask Archangel Michael to be my guide (mentor) and I wait for my higher self or Source to deliver any information I may need.

I would advise you to have a mentor present when you meditate or journey as they can give you help and advise. A mentor can be a Saint or your Guardian Angel or your deceased Grandma even, it does not matter who you choose. Just asking them in your mind is enough, saying their name three times will bring them into the scenario.

Sometimes I journey to wherever my soul wishes me to go or I consciously ask to be taken to a specific place. This could be anywhere from the top of a mountain to inside of my own body. I would not advise you to try to journey without having had some teaching or asking for a spirit to guide and teach you as was my experience. Journeying takes practise and care but once you become adept, there are no limits to inter-dimensional travel.

When I first started to meditate, I found it difficult; then I began to see coloured clouds of light and then an eye, which winked at me eventually. Seeing an eye is quite common. Apparently an open eye represents a higher level of consciousness than a closed one. Now I travel to the most amazing places and even inside my own body to balance any disharmony I find using visualisation and the power of the mind. This is often referred to as psychic surgery.

It is important to drink a glass of water after you have been meditating as it will help to ground you. Over 75% of our body is water and as we raise our vibration, it is important that we drink more of it. Eight glasses a day are recommended; it may sound like a lot but it is so important. As your body is becoming less dense and as you become lighter, the water helps you to hold more light.

Meditation Practices

By taking six slow deep breaths in to the abdomen, then six into the chest, followed by six into the upper chest, breathing through the nose and out through the mouth as mentioned earlier, you enter a meditative state. Now you can choose a subject for your meditation in order to gain insight into any illness and disharmony in the body. If you have an illness, the following is helpful to find out exactly what is causing the problem and what you need to do in order to heal yourself.

Having found a quiet place, connected to your higher self and asked your mentor to be your guide. Practice the breathing technique to take yourself into a meditative state of consciousness; you are now ready to talk to the different layers of your body, namely the physical, emotional, mental and spiritual; then for greater insight, your higher self.

As previously mentioned, we consist of various energetic layers, each one having a consciousness of its own and each one needing attention in order for us to be healthy and balanced individuals.

The following is a meditation to ask your body what it needs! Set the intention that you wish to gain insight into the particular illness or imbalance, and be specific with your intent. These are my favourite two questions:
"What do you need from me to correct the imbalance in my body" and "Do you have a message for me?"

Visualise a bright corridor with five doors, two on the left, and two on the right and one at the end. When I say visualise, I do not mean you have to see amazing visions. The images can be similar to when you are dreaming. Imagining the corridor will work just as well. Some people see their bodies as people, others just feel a presence, but both are fine. The information is the important thing, not the picture.

Walk towards the first door on your left, this is where your physical self resides. Go into the room and ask your physical self the two questions above or more if you have more. (Try not to ask too many questions as you will take hours to get to the other end of the corridor).

Wait for the reply. Because you are in an altered state of consciousness, the answer will just come into your mind, trust this process.

It is very common for the answer to be "I need love". At this point you can tell your physical self that you love them and give them a hug if necessary. You can do this in your mind by visualising it happening. Remember that all communication is telepathic when you are meditating. Thank them for the information and leave the room.

Move on to the next door on the right of the corridor; this is your emotional self. Ask the same questions and receive the answers. Thank them and move on.

Through the next door on the left is where your mental self resides, ask the same questions, receive the answers and having thanked them, move on.

The next room is your spiritual self, ask the questions and when you have received your answers, move on.

The final door is where your higher self resides. Enter the room, ask your questions and as before give thanks. Leave the room and walk back to the other end of the corridor, bringing yourself slowly back into the room you are in. Drink some water to ground yourself.

Now you have the information needed hopefully to correct the imbalance in your body. I did this to gain insight into how to balance my physical body when I was ill and the results of the meditation taught me how to resolve the problem.

Once you become more adept at this technique you will not need to do the full mediation and you can help other people gain insight about their illness or use it to help clients. For example; if you want to find out how to help a family member who is ill. You can communicate through meditation and your higher self with their physical, emotional, mental, spiritual and higher self in order to gain insight in to how to help them become balanced.

Practice your breathing to take you into a higher state of consciousness as with the meditation. Then simply ask your higher self to communicate with their higher self; then ask each individual body what it needs as you did before. You do not need to go through the corridor meditation, just ask one at a time and visualise that body in your minds eye. Remember to give thanks and move on to the next until you have the information you need.

Eventually, as you raise your vibration, you will be able to communicate with ease and no longer need the long breathing technique to connect to your higher self, it will be almost instantaneous.

Disease in the physical is usually caused by an imbalance in one or more of the other bodies (if it is not karmic or genetic). This technique can be very helpful in order to contact other parts of the human psyche such as the inner child. We can find out what the problem is and take the action needed to correct the imbalance on many levels.

Crystal Skull Meditation

One of my favourite meditations involved a crystal skull. During the meditation I could see a quartz crystal skull coming down from above my head and merging with my own skull. It felt positive and I knew I was safe. Once in position, a tube of light projected from the bottom of the skull and moved down my spine filling my whole spine with a brilliant light. A ball of it collected at my heart centre and rays of light, hundreds of them, radiated out moving around just like a laser show.

This continued for a few minutes and then stopped. I was unsure what was happening exactly but had a strong feeling of being given information that I would use at a later date. The skull disappeared as quickly as it turned up. It felt as if something had encoded my DNA; with what, who knows, however I was convinced that I had also been energetically rewired with gold wires covered in a white sheath permeating my whole body with hundreds of wires running through me just like fibre optics. It felt as if I had received a completely new nervous system.

Shortly after this I could see an image of the sphinx and a stairway leading down to an inside room. What appeared to look like a throne made of a 4ft diameter tree was in front of me and I felt the need to sit on the tree. Immediately a bright tube of light surrounded me and a large leather bound book appeared in my lap. The book opened from back to front, page by page all of its own accord, I just held it. Then the book opened again and began to flick in the opposite direction, as it did so, each page began to fill with writing. Once the book was full, the tube of light disappeared and I walked out of the room and made my way home.
I had read about the 'Mystery of the Crystal Skulls' when I was in Sri Lanka and was convinced that the skull that came to me was to do with that and that the information in it was to do with this book.

According to old Native American legends, there are 13 crystal skulls, some with movable jaws, which have the ability to heal, sing and speak; existing on Earth. Apparently they contain spiritual entities with important information about the destiny of mankind and other answers to the great mysteries of life. It is said that there are twelve, one for each of the 12 planets in the cosmos and one further skull which is vital to the whole. These skulls are in various locations, some still hidden and kept safe by the keepers, some privately owned and others housed in museums all over the world.

According to legend, it is said that one day when mankind is more evolved and pure enough to use the skulls for the highest good of all, that the skulls will be brought together and they will share their great wisdom with mankind. I look forward to that day.

29. Ancestral Healing

We are all linked to our ancestors and taking healing back through them can have excellent results regarding your healing process. It is amazing what you can inherit. Ancestral healing can also help with genetic illness depending on what the disease is.

You can invoke your ancestors to work with you. At a spiritual level, time and space impose no restrictions, so in one sense, your ancestors are living concurrently with you. Be guided by their knowledge and wisdom.

This type of healing should be done slowly and in a meditative state as a journey session would be carried out. You can tune into specific illness and who it originated from. You can carry out distant healing as you would on a living person. You may need to do a few treatments, seeking to balance emotional, mental, spiritual as well as physical. When you have completed the healing, sense or visualise it coming back through the ancestral ladder to you and if you have them, your children. You can repeat this until you feel you have balanced the energies in all of your main ancestors. As soon as you free yourself of a block, you free your children and grandchildren, if you have any.

It is possible for us to send healing back and forward seven generations or more with the intention and visualisation. Simply call in the Crystal Ki healing energies as usual, setting the intention with them that you would like to send healing back seven generations and forward seven generations through all of your direct ancestors. Remember that these energies can travel to the past and the future instantly; they are not restricted by time and space, so it is easy for them to do this.

I like to visualise myself with a separate sphere of light in front of each one of my main chakras, each one with its own wings and set the intention that each sphere will cleanse as it moves through the chakras. I then see a sphere fly through me and through a line of seven people (symbolising my ancestors) standing behind me (past) and then I see them come back the same way, clearing the chakras as they move through each person.

I then see seven people in front of me and do the same thing again, seeing the sphere of light move forward through them, clearing the chakras as they go and bringing the spheres back through to me. Remember to set the intention of the healing before you start. You can ask to heal specific problems or even karmic issues. I then send another sphere through every chakra but this time I set the intention that it is to fill the chakra with healing energy and to fill any gaps.

You can bring the grid of light through your ancestors once you become adept at the tie cutting and space clearing process. I stack the seven ancestors inside one another like the little Russian dolls and perform a distant clearing on them. You may find another visualisation that works for you.

30. Animal Medicines

It is possible according to Shamanic teachings to pull in the energetic powers of certain animals in order to gain their strengths and abilities. I have used the following simple technique of connecting with the animal kingdom for years and it has been very beneficial. All you need to do is to invoke the energy/medicine of a particular animal (or more) and that is done by simply saying the following.

"I invoke the energy of the ...." 3 times.

You can insert the name of the animal you require to help you or guide you and always remember to thank them for there help. Animals are telepathic too just like angels, so you can say it in your head and not out loud. The following animals are my favourite but you will find many others if you look up shamanic animal medicine on the internet.

Dolphin – Healing and wisdom
Dog – Loyalty and nurturing abilities
Unicorn – Enlightenment
Salmon – Strength when life feels like an uphill struggle
Duck – Nurturing abilities
Geese – Connection with Soul groups
Tiger – Seize opportunities as they arise
Spiders – Creativity
Pigeons and doves – Monogamy and love
Butterfly – Transformation
Badger – Defending ones territory when needed

Tree Medicines

We can also gain healing and wisdom by connecting with the tree medicines as we do with the animal medicines by invoking their essence with the intention to heal or meditating with them in mind.
You can invoke the essence of a particular tree by simply saying the following and inserting the name of the tree you desire to help you.

"I invoke the essence of the .... tree" 3 times.

Here are a few examples of trees healing qualities.

Holly: On an energetic level, Holly transforms our 'prickly bits' and improves our reaction to the world. Holly helps with anger, hatred, over sensitivity and aggression. It can also be used to aid catarrhal coughs and bronchial problems, flu, rheumatism and fevers. If you meditate with holly, it can aid wise choice making and calm the mind and body.

Pine: This can be used as a stimulant or tonic; it aids bladder and kidney problems and gout. Pine cones and needles were added to bath water to ease breathlessness, rheumatics and skin diseases. Pine has been used for centuries as a powerful bronchial disinfectant.

Hazel: Hazel has been used as a talisman for a healthy life. It is said to have the ability to cure fevers, excessive menstrual flow and diarrhoea. It was said to prevent toothache if you carried a double hazelnut in your pocket. Meditating upon the hazel brings the spirit alive allowing us to let go of old energy and move forward.

Silver Birch: It is said to help with spotty skin and acne, to fade freckles, to prevent stones in the kidneys and bladder when consumed as a wine. Birch is a diuretic, tonic and antiseptic. It was used to treat eczema and fevers by Gypsies and also urinary infections.

Apple: Apple trees produce a wonderful fruit and are good for constipation, fatigue, anaemia, urine retention, gastric and kidney conditions, bronchial problems, gout, hoarseness, coughs and excess cholesterol in the blood. Apple was also eaten slowly first thing in the morning to alleviate morning sickness.

Oak: Oak has many qualities and aids the soul and spirit as well as the physical body. It rebalances the patient when vital forces are strained. It is a good tonic; it was used as a snuff to stop nose bleeds. Bruised Oak leaves were also used to help ease inflammation and haemorrhoids.

Elm: Elm is used to aid purification. It is used to cleanse the skin as soap because it has astringent, anti-inflammatory qualities. Spiritually, it is used to cleanse the Spirit through meditation and if used as an incense. It induces faith in oneself. It was used to help rheumatism, ringworm and when the root was fomented, it was used to soften hard tumours.

Rowan: Rowan was said to keep witches away from you door if planted in your front garden. It helps with haemorrhoids, sore throats and inflamed tonsils. It was also used as an antibiotic. Through the visual senses it heals the human spirit. Its energy allows us to find healing, strength and purpose. Carry a twig in your pocket to help these attributes.

Willow: This is my favourite tree. Willows protect us from diseases caused by dampness. It was used to alleviate pain as an aspirin. It was said to cure barrenness and headaches. It is a good tonic as long as it is not taken more than three times per day. Willow incense aids deep emotional healing, it clears the head and lifts the spirit. It is said that one can make a wish if one dances around the Willow on the full moon.

31. To Break a Vow, Pact, Bond, Contract or Agreement

We will all have more than likely made some sort of vow, pact, bond or contract in our previous lives. These vows and the like can have serious repercussions in this life if left unbroken. If you made a past life vow of celibacy, it could affect your sex life today. Vowing to take revenge on old enemies can mean you are energetically tied to someone in this life and that connection could be draining your energy. It could mean you are tied to a group of people who are bad for you, but you find it hard to break away from them Tie cutting and breaking old vows will sort the problem out. This exercise is very useful as it terminates these vows, pacts, bonds, contracts and agreements for good. I would recommend finding a quiet place and taking some deep breaths as you would before performing the Tie Cutting exercise and then affirm the following three times……..

I call upon the presence and assistance of the Crystal Ki Energies of purification and I offer this healing for Mother Earth and all sentient beings everywhere. I break all vows, pacts, bonds, contracts and agreements that I have taken, anyone in this body has taken or anyone in my genetic lineage has taken to...INSERT FULL NAME... I declare these vows, pacts, bonds contracts and agreements null and void on all levels, past, present and future. All astral entities, all inhibitors at all dimensional levels connected with these vows, pacts, contracts and agreements must leave NOW and go into the Light if this is Gods will, you are dismissed! I ask the Crystal Ki Energies to take the vows, pacts, contracts and agreements to be burned and transmuted in the Central Flame. So be it and so it is!

Visualise this taking place until you feel they are all burned and ask the angels to let you know when they are finished. It is vital that you visualise or imagine the vows, etc, being burned. Simply saying it is not enough.

Important: Ask God and the angels to fill the voids with healing energy.

Thank God and the Crystal Ki Energies for helping you!

32. Journey Work

My son came home from school one day and said that two teachers had been following him around all day, "That's strange", I thought, and then it dawned on me that the magic mirror was trying to tell me something.

The next morning during my meditation and clearing session I could see in my minds eye two Red Indian chiefs were sitting in my lounge. They looked harmless enough, but I did a space clearing and pulled a net through the room and they both passed straight through it, so I felt sure that they were for my highest good. They both looked very impressive, with lots of feathers around their headbands, I felt quite honoured. One was in his mid thirties and the other one looked around sixty or so.

I soon realised that they were the two teachers and that they had been following me around trying to get my attention. They stayed for months and taught me how to journey through the other realms and what to look out for, the good and the bad; they told me about shape shifting and the trickster.

Tricksters can take many forms and shapes like a coyote for example. According to Native American folklore, he can take the form of any creature or messenger, he is the trickster the fool, and can be different shapes such as a man or even an animal. In some stories a trickster is a raven, they will either do you good or harm, and can lead you down the wrong path just for fun, so it is important to trust your gut instinct or intuition when journeying. If it feels suspect, it usually is.

When I journey if something I encounter feels suspect, I ask Archangel Michael (My mentor) to catch it in a Crystal Ki net of light and remove it from my path. If the net passes through it then it is okay it is no threat to me. My new guides called me Lone Tree and worked with me for a long time until I was adept at journeying. I was tested at various times, and failed sometimes but passed more than not, and felt secure with my new found skills.

When you journey inter-dimensionally, the world is your oyster, and you can travel to magical mystical places, meeting all kinds of fascinating creatures. You can become as small as a flea, or hold the whole planet in your hand. There are no limits, and because of the diversity of this practice I journeyed often, and learnt many things.

I journey my clients and take them to various places, some may need to go into a secret garden to meet another soul who will talk to them and give them advice. Others may journey inside of there own body to help find out what is causing the imbalance and find a healing solution. Some of these sessions are very Dr Who and great fun. I am a guide and help my clients find what they need but their inner wisdom is in control of where they travel to and what they find when they get there.

33. Crystal Ki Healing – Case Studies & Soul Retrieval

Sarah was 39 years old and recovering from cancer of the cervix. Sarah was very down and during her first treatment with me. I noticed black serpent type energy in her sacral and promptly removed it using a net of light, it even hissed at me when I pulled it out of her chakra.

I generally perform a tie cutting at the start of treatments and on the second treatment with Sarah I began to notice a spirit around her that was not for her highest good. When I journeyed her she could see a man, he looked quite dark to me and I did a tie cutting to remove him. Sarah did not find him a threat but I was not sure about him at all. There was also a tall gold light being with her, who looked to be extra-terrestrial but he was very light and obviously a good soul, he appeared every time she came to see me. He must have been one of her guides; he had a calm presence about him.

On Sarah's third treatment we decided that we should perform a soul retrieval, I explained to her what this meant and advised her that the process could not be rushed. I explained that it would be vital to her healing process to work towards finding the soul fragmentation: this is the part of our essence or subconscious (in her case, her inner child) that has been lost or locked itself away due to some kind of trauma or upset. It is vital that when you find the lost soul fragment, you ask them what they need and meet their request, before they can be integrated back into the heart of the client. This lost soul fragment can be an adult part of us but in my experience I have found that people I deal with usually have a small child that needs to be returned.

The aim is to integrate that child essence back into the heart chakra of the client, allowing them to let go of the past and to feel whole again, it is a process that can have profound effects.

Sarah continued to come to me for a few weeks and on the fifth treatment I recommended that she took some flower essences remedies to help aid her with the recovery and to release old energy from the system. By the sixth treatment she looked bright and happy when she arrived. However she had been reading about cancer and the causes of it, as she had wanted to know why she had contracted cancer in the first place, I tried to explain that it was linked to her childhood, but she needed confirmation, so before we journeyed, we set the intention that the answer was to be found today. She eventually saw her younger self hiding in a wardrobe.

I explained to her that we would be able to speak using telepathy to this part of her psyche and that we needed to integrate the frightened child back into her heart chakra in order to return this soul fragment to where it was meant to be. But we had difficulty in reassuring the child that she would be loved and would be safe if she came back into adult Sarah's heart. I explained that she would be safe and that Sarah's heart was full of love and a beautiful place to be. The whole process was quite strange for Sarah but I had done this many times before and she was amazed that when she asked the little girl if she could hear me she said yes, even though all communication at soul level was done telepathically. I would speak to adult Sarah but use telepathy to communicate to her inner child.

Within ten minutes the child Sarah was back home within adult Sarah's heart, right where she belonged and I could see her dancing and skipping in my minds eye as I poured more love energy into Sarah's heart chakra.

Little Sarah only looked around 5 years old with her hair plaited, and wearing a pretty dress with baby doll shoes, she held a toy doll in her hands. I explained this to adult Sarah and praised child Sarah for helping big Sarah to grow and healing her, and the little girl even blew me a kiss.

Sarah was still unclear as to what caused her cancer and I took it upon myself to ask why as a child she would hide in a wardrobe. She said it was because her mother would say that she was going to put her into a home. We had already cut ties with her mum which had helped with the healing process. Threatening a child like that, can be traumatic enough to trigger one bad cell memory; that cell can lay dormant for years but then turn cancerous later in life. The whole process of finding your soul and forgiving all concerned is important in order to release the root cause of the disease. The cancer formed in her emotional chakra which makes sense. Sarah needed to go home and assimilate the whole thing and I explained that she might feel emotional for a week or two as the returned soul fragment settles in. It was also important to feed the newly integrated child with some childish fun to make her feel at home.

The next client I would like to tell you about was Kim, her mother had advised her to book an appointment with me. When she arrived she was very low and she had a victim consciousness (e.g. Why me…. I always get the bad luck etc), This woman was only in her thirties but was in a bad way and in the first visit I felt the need to do a Tie Cutting from her ex-boyfriend in order to free her from him energetically. I explained about victim consciousness and negative thinking only created more negativity. She was a bright woman and seemed to understand and grasp what I was saying, immediately. Kim was one of those people you can easily take a shine too, she was a likable soul.

I balanced her head and heart chakras; her head was full of negative thought forms, entities and belief systems and it took me some time to clear it, but I knew she was going to need more treatments and a soul retrieval very quickly after talking to her at the initial consultation. I needed to get her into a better mindset and I explained to her that positive attracts positive and negative attracts negative. I would spend extra time talking to her and teaching her about the how we create our lives with our thoughts and feelings. She grasped the advice and put it into practise; she bought the movie "The Secret" and soon began to fly.

The change was amazing; she was smiling and confident, even optimistic after only two treatments. By the third visit she had met a new man, a good man, but her old way of victim thinking was starting to creep back in so we decided she needed to do a tie cutting with that part of herself, namely her self saboteur. Kim was shocked when she saw her darker self in the visualisation; we cut ties with her, asking the Universe to send her the new happy version. She could see the new her walking towards her, hugging her and absorbing the new her into her body; with that, we had brought in the shining positive Kim and integrated her new essence.

Kim went on to start telling others about positive thinking after only two or three treatments herself, she was a quick learner and I enjoyed working with her. By the fourth treatment she was happy, still with her new man, and really positive in her attitude.

Kim told me how her stepmother would lock her in a cupboard in the dark when they were little and now I know why she had problems with men as she blamed her father as he was not around when this was going on. Men treated Kim badly because she had victim mentality. If you see yourself as a victim the Universe will send you people who will abuse you and treat you badly. You create your abuser! It is your fault. Only you can change your situation by changing your negative thinking and belief systems.

Kim told me that she hated her stepmother and I explained that hate is so powerful that it will keep her attached to this woman in this and the next life, or until she forgives her. I asked her to forgive the soul if she could not forgive the personality, with the soul being the pure part of her essence, and with that in mind I took her through the process of cutting the ties, and she cut them with ease.

The strangest thing however happened at the beginning of Kim's journey when she was walking through a wood, and she saw this woman keep popping her head out from behind the trees. I told her that the woman (her stepmother) wanted to help her find her soul fragment and help her to heal and repair the damage. Kim accepted this and she agreed to hold hands with this woman to my amazement as only ten minutes ago, she said that she hated her. They both went into a small house in the woods where the child Kim was waiting, sitting on the floor.

Kim's inner child would not talk or look the adult Kim in the eye, she would not hug her and was angry with adult Kim, she was very unhappy. I thought we may have a problem with this one, so I decided to do a tie cutting and clear the energy between them. This helped and the child Kim decided to reunite if adult Kim would promise her safety and love, which adult

Kim did and the child Kim jumped back into the heart chakra in a flash. This was fairly straight forward soul retrieval

I never heard more about Kim until a month after this when a good friend of mine who know Kim's family said that they had seen a great improvement in such a short period of time. She was much happier and optimistic and no longer had the victim mentality, which I was pleased to hear. Kim was so impressed with her treatments that she decided to do two workshops with me. She now has a much brighter outlook on life.

During one treatment she was having with me, she was shown her past and her future and in her future she could see herself in a lovely home, happily married with a man she truly loved, and with another child, a vision which made her very happy.

Another client, Rob, came to see me upon recommendation from two friends of his, both of them knew me, and one of them was a nurse who also understood how the Crystal Ki energy works. He was about to go into hospital to have one of his kidneys removed as he was suffering from kidney and lung cancer. He was only in his forties.

We had time to do three treatments before his operation and he responded extremely well to the sessions. I also visited him after his operation when he was in intensive care, giving him a treatment whilst he was unconscious by channelling Crystal Ki energy through his hand into his body. The energy that went through me was ice cold and looked like clear diamonds, it was the highest vibrational energy I had ever seen, let alone channelled. Although he was very ill he did pull through and was soon home.

He came to the clinic regularly for chakra clearing and journey sessions and we always started with a tie cutting to get rid of any worry or fear that was hanging around him, but Rob loved journeying the most. He was very visual and could journey very well, he picked up messages and visuals from his higher self easily and he was a fearless traveller and a joy to work with, if only all clients were as easy.

His main blocks were his throat, heart and sacral chakras. His throat chakra was connected to him swallowing his words and being too nice to say what he actually thought, he needed to speak his truth more. His heart chakra was all about him not loving and forgiving himself for past mistakes. His sacral chakra was connected to all of these emotional issues that were suppressed and then being stored in that part of the body, he needed to release his emotions more freely.

Rob was quite a thinker and had problems with his root chakra also because that became blocked as a result of not being grounded. I told Rob he needed to get outside more and connect with Mother Earth in order to ground his mental energy.

During one of his journeying sessions Rob noticed black lines, like string being removed from his chest while I was clearing that area with my hands. On another occasion we saw an angel clear a patch of dark energy from his stomach. This was good news and we were both pleased when we had witnessed it. Dark energy can show up as brown or black to someone who can see it with clairvoyant vision or using the minds eye.

Cancer has a frequency or vibration as does everything in the physical world. The lower vibrations being more solid and hence physical and the higher being more pure and spiritual. The frequency of cancer is not compatible with the physical body and it will devour the cells accordingly. These low frequency diseases can manifest as a result of long term negative emotional states of mind such as being frightened, envious, judgemental, angry, unforgiving, worried, etc. These feelings create low frequency vibrations and can be damaging to the health.

And because how you feel inside is reflected into your reality, your perception will be one of problems as your whole life is affected by this negative mind set and energy. It can not only damage your health but your relationships and even your career. The trick is to recognise this negative mental attitude, then to take action to put it right by taking responsibility for your mind and your thoughts. Try to stop seeing yourself as a victim of life and set the intention to see yourself as getting better every day, then act upon that intention starting with positive thinking and a better diet as good food has a massive effect on our mental health. Let go of any guilt as it is self destructive and work towards raising your frequency in the physical, emotional, mental and spiritual levels. Happiness and balance will change things rapidly.

We were often shown words when Rob journeyed such as hope, power, trust, and even optimism once, so even though he was quite ill, he felt sure he would pull through and he was quite an enlightened soul as he knew the illness was teaching him something. I confessed that I thought he would heal much better if he was away from his relatives as they were so fearful and worried about him, that they would drag him down when they visited him by bringing that low energy with them. He was very sensitive to energy and I advised him to get outside in the garden or go out into the park to get some fresh air and blow away the cobwebs.

His illness did get worse for a while, but then he began to make rapid progress and as he is a light worker himself, I feel that he has important work to do when he recovers; I could sense that when we first met and I am pleased to report Rob is still doing really well.

Another girl in her thirties who came to me needing a soul retrieval and we came across the lost part of her soul in a different way than was usual. I generally would come across a key in the journey process and then would unlock a cage or box to find the soul fragment, there was no key or a cage or anything like that. This lost part of her, the young girl, just walked up to her when she was on a beach in the meditation that we were doing as part of the treatment, and she could see this young girl walking towards her and she realised it was her when she was nine years old.

It was different to previous experiences and when this young girl was asked what it was she needed she insisted that the now older her had a dance with her on the beach which my client found very strange. She danced in the sand, just as the young girl wanted as she needed to let her inner child play, and have fun, to lighten up, laugh and reconnect with the child like side of her nature. So she visualised this happening, and danced and sang with the younger version of herself and within no time at all as she embraced that child and that part of her, it was then integrated into her heart chakra with great ease. This was simple soul retrieval.

I have also worked with re-birthing and an example of this was experienced with a woman who was 30 years old. She had issues with moving forward in her life and felt something was blocking her, and this was causing her anxiety problems because of her lack of direction. A few people had mentioned to her that she could possibly benefit by going through a re-birthing process. I offered her my assistance and gave her some back ground on my experience and knowledge. Due to the fact that she was so anxious I visited her at home and began to work with her.

Starting with the breathing techniques that I use to take her into a semi-meditative state of consciousness, I took her down visually in a lift and into the womb where she stayed for a few minutes. I asked her if she was alright and she said that she felt a little nervous and wanted someone with her. We decided to call on the soul of her sister who she was very close to, they were best friends. Being inside the womb with her sister holding her hand, she felt much more stable and she felt happier to move forward. So when she was ready I asked her to visualise a doorway and for her to walk through it. Beyond the door was a long curvy tube much like you would imagine the birth canal would be. When she got to the end there was another doorway and beyond that a beautiful room with a big bed and couch; the whole room was yellow and gold.

Once in the room, I asked her if she needed anything and she said she wanted to go and lie down. I let her relax and rest for a while. When she was ready I guided her awareness back into the bedroom and it was over, the re-birthing was complete.

From what I have been told, she is happy and getting on with her life. Apparently she is now learning about angel therapies and crystal therapies and is quite enlightened in that respect.

34. Soul Purpose

Many of us when we get older will look back and see what we have achieved, or in some cases, what we haven't. It is important to have put something into this world and we all have a purpose, with each soul having its own personal mission. It may be simply to learn gratitude and forgiveness or to become a spiritual teacher or even a world leader, who knows? I believe my purpose is to be a teacher, teaching about healing, self purification and spiritual growth and this book is an important part of that purpose. The tie cutting and energy clearing is very special and powerful information and this was the best way to get it out into the world.

Movies and books like "The Secret" inform us about the laws of attraction and teach us to have gratitude for the many blessings we have in our lives, but if your goal is greatly different from the plan your soul had for you before you were born, then you are less likely to achieve them, so it is important for you to find out what your soul purpose is and take steps towards making more achievable goals.

Your soul is your self-aware essence of your being and is the true basis of your wisdom. Your soul is immortal and therefore existed prior to each incarnation and lifetime. With each life you will have a new agenda based on your soul's growth in a previous incarnation and we are all here to learn and grow. Some of us however have more active roles than others, whereas some just go along with their job and their home life without really questioning and if asked were they happy, they would say "yeah my life is okay", but is that really enough? Do you really just want an okay life? If it could be better would you change it? Or would you carry on and ignore your hearts desires? There is no need to strive to be a world leader if you don't want to but at least settle for something that makes you happy, something that makes your heart sing.

We are not here to just survive, and discovering our true purpose is important because when we live our truth we evolve, life has more meaning, we become more creative and we live with a higher level of awareness and integrity.

If you find out that your soul purpose is very important and you find the thought of it overwhelming, don't worry. Apparently there are three souls incarnate and assigned to each important purpose, so if you do not want to go ahead with your specific soul purpose, there is someone else who will. The job will get done and you do not need to feel guilty because you changed your mind. The Universe is in control of all eventualities, so worry not.

There are many books and CD's on the market that can help you to decide what your purpose is and if you choose to discover more you may find yourself embarking on a journey that will be transformative and empowering.

Many years ago, a lady I met told me that I was a medium and a clairvoyant. I was also told that I would be involved in public speaking. At the time I was sceptical and did not take a lot of notice but a year ago I spoke at the Leamington Spa Peace festival to thousands of people. I was terrified but I faced my fear and took the microphone and stood on the band stand and spoke about peace and self healing. The words seemed to channel through me from another source and it just flowed. The lady was right and I have spoken to other groups since then and I really enjoy it. Because of this experience I now believe that public speaking is also an important part of my purpose and look forward to talking to more audiences in the near future.

35. 3rd Dimensional Signs

When I began to work with angels and spirit guides, there was always a part of my logical mind that questioned the guidance I was getting, or put it down to an over imaginative mind. The logical (left) side of my brain was well developed; maths and science came easy to me, my job as a draughtsperson proved that. The intuitive and creative (right) side of my brain, the more feminine aspect needed to be developed further, and I did not feel comfortable trusting my intuition initially.

I had begun to develop many of the psychic senses such as clairvoyance, which is vision using the minds eye and also images and messages in the physical world, the 3rd dimension. Clairsentience which means you feel people's emotions. Claircognizance is receiving messages in the forms of thoughts directly into the mind. Clairaudience means receiving guidance in the form of verbal messages either in your mind or with your ears directly from spirit and clairomniscience which relates to instant knowingness.

With all of these senses blossoming my life began to get busy very quickly, and I was still finding my feet so I was a little apprehensive until someone prompted me to ask my guides to use another form of communication – what a brilliant idea that was! I did this, and I happened upon some information that mentioned different types of clairvoyance depending upon what frequency the medium was tuned into.

There was a form of clairvoyance which meant you could see things in the 3rd dimension or physical world. In the film Bruce Almighty, Bruce, the lead character asked for a sign from God and a truck full of road traffic signs pulls out in front of his car. He certainly got his sign but he did not see it.

Once I realised that I had this type of clairvoyance as well I was flying, signs were everywhere, it was just superb. I would notice them on the side of white vans, on number plates and t-shirts, just to name a few. I would hear things three times and people would give me messages without even realising that they were doing it. I really began to tune into this frequency, and boy did my life change for the better. I had a communication method I trusted as back up that worked in unison with my guides. It was great, if not a little bizarre.

It took about a year until I had a good substantial assortment of what I now see as my library of visual aids and divine messages. Working at this level meant that I was seeing miracles everyday and my confidence levels grew and grew as a result.

One day I was driving home from my friends. I had been for a treatment, I had been crying and was angry about how I had been treated and misjudged by certain people. My thymus or higher heart chakra had been open for a while but I felt it closing down because of the anger I was feeling, I even had a pain in my chest because of it. During my journey home a white van cut me up, so I had no choice but to see it and I noticed that the words written on the side, in big green letters said "Panic". Green is a colour associated with the heart chakra and I immediately knew I needed to do some work on healing my higher heart chakra to release the negative feelings that were crushing me. So when I arrived home I did a healing meditation and I could see an arrow piercing right through my heart which was removed by my angels, this alleviated the pain immediately.

You are probably thinking where did that come from? Over the years I have removed what looked like arrows, swords, daggers, anchors, shackles, metal plates, hooks, chains, black symbols and an assortment of moving manifested energy from either myself, my friends, or clients. The one thing I have been guided to do is to not analyse where most of these things come from. The images are symbolic of negativity, that's all I need to know. Some will have come from past lives, some from psychic attacks, even to the point of attacking ourselves and holding ourselves back. Some are astral inhibitors, so my advice is try not to over analyse, you could end up paranoid, just let it go and you'll be fine.

I was in the process of buying my new property and I was driving home from my voluntary work at the local hospital. I asked my angels if there was anything else I needed to do when I got home other than the mental list I had already made. A bird flew straight across my windscreen; this is always a sign that a message is on the way from the Universe. Immediately after that I saw a white van with these letters on the side "BYBOXB48AM" I read it as Buy Box before 8am, which I saw as a reminder to call the estate agents with some urgent information they had requested before 8am the next morning, I thanked my angels and rang the estate agents as soon as I got home.

I had more or less given up smoking but one evening, I asked my boyfriend to go and buy me a packet of cigarettes from the local shop. He was also able to read the 3rd dimensional signs especially the ones on cars. When he came back he was excited at what he had seen outside the shop. There had been a car parked with a private number plate of NICOTX – what a blatant sign to give up smoking. It was still a while before I stopped smoking altogether. It took me seven attempts before I gave up, so stick at it if you are trying to kick the habit, as seven attempts is apparently the average. Smoking really damages your light as well as your health.

Other messages were hearing or seeing broken glass three times, if you notice this happening, check to see if you have been enclosed in a force field or glass box, it sounds crazy but it can happen. Blocks can develop way out in your aura and form a shield of energy which can hold us back. I regularly check my aura is clear, right out to level 35 as egg shaped clouds of contaminated energy can form and can cause problems. I once found a layer of muddy cloud like energy around a lady outside of her God layer (layer 33) and I considered this cloud to be layer 34, in order to clear it I needed to surround it with the grid of light and that is why I use grids to layer 35 now.

Alarms going off in the street or sirens are always a sign that something negative is around either me or my client, and this usually means a tie cutting or space clearing needs to be carried out. Dripping taps and leaks mean unshed tears, flat tyres mean you are a bit deflated, with me the left tyres mean emotionally, and the right physically. If there is low frequency energy in my home which can come through via T.V or visitors, light bulbs will blow, and if that happens I clear the space immediately. Unless you ban all of the sex and violence on TV or on computer games, stop people coming into your home and live like a monk, it is virtually impossible to keep the lower frequency energy out of your space, so it is important to cleanse your home on a regular basis. The technique I have given previously can be used on your home and your garden, I advise you to take the grid to the boundaries of your property.

If a bird or butterfly flies close to you it means that a message is on the way from the Universe, so be aware of any guidance you feel you are getting although it can take a while to learn to read and notice these 3D signs. I recommend watching Bruce Almighty on DVD; it is a very clever film, full of important messages about using and abusing your power and being responsible. The children will love it too; it is really funny. As we raise our vibration, we become more powerful and it is important to know that with greater power comes greater responsibility and greater karmic consequences.

There have been times when I have had my brow chakra (third eye) blocked by outside influences. The sign for this is sunglasses when there is no sun shine, the dark glasses just catch your attention or I notice headbands and blindfolds. The blocks can look like sink plugs, metal bands or material tied around my head. When I meditate and see what is blocking my third eye I visualise my angels taking it away, it is important, that you visualise it being removed in order to clear it.

Once again, I do not analyse where it came from or if it's some ones fault, as it is usually to do with the energy attached to them and without their knowledge. Even a family member or your dearest best friend can have something negative attached to them. Usually I will notice a change in mood when someone has something attached to them. People get entities attached to them regularly (you can pick them up in the supermarket) and a tie cutting usually removes most things easily. They are just like flees and are attracted to clean people, so if you have one, don't take it personally, just remove it using the technique described earlier.

My usual warning for general rubbish is the two colours red and black. I can be driving along and my eyes will be drawn to someone wearing red and black. Black is the sign for something more sinister such as entities or negative spirit attachments, if they are to my left it means that my energy needs cleansing or there is lower octane stuff at my destination. If it is on the right it means that it is connected to someone else perhaps someone I am thinking of or the person I am on my way to visit. If you see red and black please don't panic, it's just my sign to clear energy and it's become a daily part of my life now. These signs are from my library, yours could be something different altogether.

You may be thinking okay, but there is red and black all over the place, that's true, but for me it's the ones that stand out and people who draw your attention or you feel like you have had a tap on the shoulder, you will know when it happens. When I hear the word red or scarlet, it usually means "stop". If I am in a car and a red car cuts me up, it reminds me to change my thoughts from what I am thinking about or to stop what I am about to do. If I see a picture or hear the name of the same animal three times in the day it means I need to invoke that animal and pull in its energy to help me. They all mean different things as I mentioned earlier and the animal kingdom are also there to help you in spirit.

Whenever there are planetary changes occurring, like mother earths chakras being activated, I usually get together with a few friends and we meditate to help with these changes. One day when I was in town and it said "stop naked" I knew that it was a message for me to be celibate for a while before the meditation;

the vital energy that you emit when you climax actually weakens your spiritual creative power, thus affecting the power I bring to the meditation.

The way to still hold your power is to allow the energy to go from you into your partner up their spine through their heart and into yours, take it in a figure of eight up through your spine out through the top of your head and into their crown, down through their head, spine then their heart through to your heart and back down to your spine into your sacral. Just set the intention and visualise it happening, then you are not losing your vital life force. I remember watching a TV program about Chinese emperors which stated that they did not allow themselves to climax during intercourse and this was because they lost energy (Chi) and hence spiritual power as a result.

When I was recently on holiday I visited a lovely 5 star hotel spa for a massage; we were treated like royalty. For a couple of days later after this massage I had stomach problems and it began to feel really uncomfortable and bloated. I was in the supermarket and I asked my guides what was causing it, my eyes were then directed to a shelf that had three bottles on it with cobras on the labels. I had removed lots of snake type energies from my clients and I knew that this was what I needed to do to myself back at the hotel. I asked my higher self where this had come from, and I was directed to a label that said Cleopatra it was then I realised that I had picked this bad energy up in the spa; its name was Cleopatra Spa. I soon removed it using a Crystal Ki net of light and my stomach settled immediately.

In early 2008 I was feeling particularly stressed with certain global transitional problems and I called out loud in frustration as I was driving my car home, "Why did God choose me for this particular job?" Seconds later a huge fruit and vegetables lorry passed and the words on the side said "Well Picked", that really made me laugh and I felt so much better. God really does work in mysterious ways.

Basically reading the 3rd dimensional signs is a very personal thing and anything you see or hear three times is a sign from the Universe but try to take notice of things you see on the side of vans, it could help you on your journey. I am very grateful for my 3D signs and messages but my intuition is really good now and I am also guided by spirit.

36. Television and Radio

Television and radio can damage the soul and as you develop spiritually your chakras will become more sensitive as a higher frequency of light is present in your body. Once you have stimulated your chakras and activated your DNA changes, you have become a higher density light being and this means that you need to take care of these chakras and your aura by keeping it clear of lower vibrational energy. Cleaning your energetic body will be like cleaning your teeth, a matter of routine.

Performing regular space clearing on your home will be just as important. Everything electrical allows energy into your home, that means your T.V., telephone, electrical appliances, computer etc. These objects can also allow darker energies into your home acting as portals to them and it is important to clear it on a regular basis.

You may be clairsentient and able to pick up the vibes, but if you are not there is no need to worry, as by using the space clearing technique in this book you can clear your whole house and your place of work in minutes. Remember to do your place of work at night when no one is in the building.

The old fashioned way of clearing was to burn sage and herbs, etc. but I find the net of light works for me and it doesn't run the risk of burning my carpet or smelling as bad as burning sage. Playing some classical music and opening the windows regularly will always help.

Many of these lower energies enter our home via the television, and the energy they attract is the same low frequency. This is why a lot of people who sit in front of the television day and night become depressed and docile. They really need to get outside to get some fresh air in order to clear that negative energy away and clear their minds. I believe TV is a form of mind control wrapped in a pretty box and can damage the subconscious mind. Watching sex, violence, horror movies and worst of all the news, this is full of doom and gloom and creates anger and sadness in the viewer. I've heard that in America, the average child has seen over 12,000 murders on TV and Cable TV by the time they are 14 years old. We allow TV to pollute children's minds and then we are shocked when they are violent as a result. It's crazy.

We are highly influenced by what we see and our soul is an innocent child being polluted by what we witness. Do you want to damage your soul in this way? Although your conscious mind knows that this is just a movie, your subconscious will record it as violence and will store that negativity in your mind not differentiating between the conscious and subconscious reality; in this case it's not just a movie, your subconscious mind can just recall the violence as normal behaviour.

Too much negative input not only damages your soul, but it damages you and your children. If you find yourself in a situation when you are watching something which you believe is damaging in this way, why not turn it over to another channel, or better still, switch it off altogether and go and do something healthy and fun instead.

We become what we think about most of all, and our thoughts create our experiences. If we think about collective negative mindsets which attract more of the same then forming into a huge mass of low frequency energy. We will realise that we are making the planet a lower frequency than it should be. The whole world becomes affected by lower energies, so if you must watch it then try and watch pre-recorded films etc, where you can be assured of its content as that can be less damaging than live television.

It is also worth considering that people who keep their children locked indoors stuck in front of a television or computer screen thinking they are keeping them safe from the dangers outside are probably causing them more harm as it would be healthier to go out riding a bike, playing in the fresh air and getting some exercise. So many children look pale and over weight due to their unhealthy lifestyles. I ask Archangel Michael to guide and protect my son when he goes out and then I just have faith that he will be safe. If you fear for your children, you send that energy into their lives, you can cause them more harm than good by worrying about them.

A friend's young son is addicted to playing computer games, he is as white as a ghost and always complaining as these games are causing him so much harm and distress and his parents cannot even see it. The games he plays are always making him feel inadequate because he cannot always reach the next level. He can become aggressive and sometimes violent when his parents try to turn the games off at bedtime. This is just terrible and I feel it is important that the general public should be constantly warned against the prolonged use of playing computer games. The warnings at present are not sufficient.

I also feel the same way about children using mobile phones, its killing them with kindness in my opinion, and buying them expensive phones is madness, you may as well buy them a t-shirt which says "Come and mug me, please" in huge letters. Apart from that cell phones emit radiation into our brains. This is particularly bad for young children under the age of 10 years old. Parents should investigate further before handing out these killer gifts.

37. Developing Spiritual Growth

There are many ways to develop spiritual growth, spending time alone, reading, maybe listening to some e-books or CDs, having a good look at yourself really, and looking in the mirror of consciousness, because what is going on around you is a reflection of what is going on inside of you. So if you are experiencing bad things in your life, maybe you need to take a look deep within yourself and see what is going on and to get some help to repair the damage because, "As within so without".

I once went on a three day retreat which really helped me move forward. Before then I never really considered myself to be a teacher, but after this experience I realised that teaching at a spiritual and energetic level is something I could do. I found out that my strengths were helping others to look at the bigger picture, to open their minds and just see the vastness of it all. To help people to realise, we are the painter, the paint and the canvas. I had gone with a friend and by the end of the first day we seemed to have formed a small group of people who came together and connected with us because they wanted to talk to us or we would pick up on information that they needed intuitively. This group inspired me to write my first workshop.

When I run workshops teaching tie cutting and space clearing for example, I do try to raise the level of consciousness in the group I am teaching. We look at everything, not just removing negative energies from our space or negative spirit releasement, but also information relating to the bigger picture. I talk about why we have so many holistic healing therapies these days and why we need to make good use of them. I make them aware that we need to cleanse ourselves and the planet. We talk about soul refinement and working towards 2012 and the ascension process of the whole planet. When my students leave, they go away a bit more enlightened and I get a great sense of satisfaction which I could not really find in doing anything else. I have come across some interesting books on my path, I am always looking on the internet to see what I can find and asking for the Divine Truth so that I find the right information and more often than not that has been the case.

I am always learning something, I enjoy learning and even if I do not understand things with my conscious mind, I know that my soul understands it all. Feeding your soul is the way forward and hopefully this book will help. I do question everything, and I am not easily misled by any means. I use meditation daily to speak to my guides and my higher self, so I am a lot happier and willing to put these words out into the world whereas before I was still not quite sure if I should really be doing this, even though I kept hearing the words book, book, book, and ink, ink, ink, which was the Universe guiding me to do it..

38. The Divine Truth and Prayer

I like to start my day with giving thanks for the peaceful night sleep I have had, I also like to state that I am a channel of love and light in order that I do not use my own energy when working on people. I ask God to place a 1 metre wide orb of protective light around my earth star chakra to act as a filter for energies coming up from the earth and request that it is camouflaged to protect it. I also ask for this protective orb to be placed around my son's earth star chakra.

I ask God to guide and protect me to ensure that all energies, entities and information I receive come from the Divine and no other. I ask God to bless my home and family. Then I give my day to God and the Angels and let it all go. Having lit a candle I am ready to do my morning clearing and meditation session after which I close all of my chakras both front and back and ask my higher self to choose the protection I need for my physical body if I am going out. Usually it is a layer of light and a layer of camouflage on each level.

I have heard many spiritual teachers say to their students "go out and shine your light", however I feel guided to camouflage mine and I notice that if I don't, people tend to stare at me in the street. It also keeps the moths away, so to speak, as they are very attracted to the light and have helped themselves to my energy in the past, so I now keep it under wraps and I suggest you do the same.

At night I say thank you for the abundance in my life and I visualise my chakras being locked and a special sleep pod forming around me, which is also camouflaged on the outside. I ask my Guardian Angel to watch over my physical body while I sleep and I say the following affirmation..... "I command that while my body sleeps my astral body will travel only to the higher planes of divine light, so be it and so it is."

This allows me to bridge the lower planes where all of the lower energies are. When we are asleep at night we astral project (go out of body) and it is important to protect your physical body from nosey spirits and negative energies that can arise, by asking your Guardian Angel to keep watch over it for you.

I then finish with this prayer..... "Dear God, I ask to see, hear, know, think and feel the Divine Truth, to sense beyond all illusion and delusion. I ask God and the angels to remove all doubts and fears from my mind, body and soul as I sleep; I give thanks for my life and all life, Amen."

Once this is done I feel content to go to sleep and have noticed if I forget I have a restless night and problems can occur as a result.

Asking for the Divine Truth is important; many books and gurus advise us to seek the truth. The wording is critical as there is a difference between the truth and the divine truth. Consider this, if you have ten people all from similar backgrounds and you sit them in front of a movie and ask them to write a page about the films true meaning. I can assure you what you will get are ten different versions of how they perceived the films truth to be. As each persons truth will be dependant on where they are in their life journey with the unhappy people writing about the negative aspects in the movie and the positive people will write about the positive aspects. They are all the truth, but only from their perception and hence, not the divine truth. The Divine Truth is Gods version, the enlightened version of Truth.

A lot of books are filled with the author's truth and perspective as it was at that point in their life journey. These are ego based in general. That is why I wanted to wait until now to write this book. As I have transcended many levels of ego although I do have an ego, it keeps me human but I am very enlightened and happy with the information I have written.

Spiritually I am now in a high level of consciousness and have been finding Divine Truths for years and I am satisfied with my findings. I still have much to learn, however, I also could not write these words if I did not believe them myself, but I still urge you to carry out your own search for Divine Truth. There is only one Divine Truth and when we find it, we attain self realisation and start to prepare for the next step in our spiritual evolution through other planes of existence.

39. Universal Spiritual Laws

One of the most important things I have learned on my journey so far is about Universal Spiritual Laws. There are according to Diana Cooper's brilliant book, "A little light on Spiritual Laws", 36 spiritual laws which govern all of life on Earth (I highly recommend this book). I will talk about a few of my favourites as they have taught me so much about my self and the people around me. This book also contains vital information to help you learn about the mystery school we live in from how it all works as a mirror to teach us about our own short comings, to creating abundance, good karma and much more. This book is the first one I recommend my students buy as it has changed my life and it could change yours too. Here are just a few of my favourite laws.

The Law of Reflection - This explains that the Universe and life as we know act a magic mirror, reflecting back at us the true aspects of ourselves we need to address and improve or not as the case may be. The outer world or reality reflects our life and what we need to learn about the shadow self. The people you like are mirroring aspects of yourself that are positive and the people you don't like are mirroring the part of yourself that your soul is trying to bring to your attention. When you are aware, you can alter your negative behaviour to suit. You will attract people to you that mirror your attributes be they good or bad. Like attracts like. Look at the people you do not like and look at yourself, the mirror never lies.

For example, if your lover is arrogant and maybe drinks too much alcohol, ask yourself "Am I arrogant and do I drink too heavily? Is your child always in trouble at school? Are you behaving badly and this is being reflected in your child's behaviour? Are your taps leaking or have you had a flood recently in your home? These things represent unshed tears and emotions that are being kept inside. These can lead to serious disease in the body. So get a good sad movie and cry, cry, cry. The tap will probably stop dripping (mine did). Has everyone you bumped into today been angry? Maybe you need to deal with your own anger issues? If you notice people limping, maybe you need more balance in your life?

Do you see how it works? Everything we need to know is right there in front of us when we take notice and become more aware.

The Law of Attraction - This law is simple, we attract that which we think about most. The movie "The Secret" is all about this law. If you are a negative person, you will attract negative people and situations into your daily life. If you are the kind of person that talks about your friends behind their backs, don't be surprised when you find out they have been talking about you. Your actions are being mirrored by them. Gossip is a very bad thing and causes a lot of pain. It is your fault, not theirs.

If you pick fault with yourself or see yourself as a victim you will attract people who will pick on you and act out the victimiser. YOU made yourself the victim. Change the way you look at things and the things will change the way they look.

On the other hand if you are a kind, positive person, you will attract similar and have a happy life. If you have a dream, you will attract people and situations that will help you to achieve that dream. One step at a time.

The Law of Projection - This law is about us projecting our beliefs onto other people. If you have a bad experience with a particular relationship for example, you decide that all men/woman are bad and tell everyone this, you are projecting your belief onto others. You have created a negative belief system in your mind and are spreading wrong information. This can cause a lot of damage as some people are very vulnerable and will believe the same, thus spreading negative information that will attract more bad partners to you and those who believed your statement.

We project our good and bad attributes onto other people by saying things like "You must feel terrible about your ex", because we feel terrible and expect them to feel the same when it is not always the case. Statements like "Everyone loves chocolate!" and "Everyone hates spiders!" are again projections of beliefs. Both statements are incorrect.

When we fall in love, we project that love onto one another and cannot see any short comings in the other person. As the relationship moves on we see deeper aspects of ourselves projected in the other and believe them to be their negative or positive attributes, but truly they are ours, not theirs. They are only acting as a mirror.

The Law of Resistance - This law is about pushing away things we really want. We do this by using words like, don't, can't, won't, etc. The conscious mind can assimilate these negative words but the subconscious mind does not recognise them at all.

If you say "don't drop that cup" to a child, the child's subconscious mind will hear "drop that cup", it is better to say, "take care with that cup". Use positive phrases and leave the negative words out. We all say things like "don't forget to put the cat out please" to our partners for example. However their subconscious mind will hear "forget to put the cat our please" and come to bed leaving the cat to have a party. Changing the way we talk to one another is vital and in that instance a better phrase to use would be "remember to put the cat out please".

We must leave out the negative connotations to master this law and saying things like "I don't want to be single" will keep you single. Concentrate on saying "I would love to meet my soul mate" and see how things change. We resist success by saying "I can't stand this job". We resist having a loving relationship by saying "I am never going to meet the right person". We resist being happy by saying "I am so unhappy", and your statements create your experience. It is possible to turn things around by saying more positive things like "I am healthy, wealthy and wise" and therefore cover all areas.

The Law of Prayer - The law of Prayer is about asking for your desires, believing that they are on their way and also showing gratitude for the blessings you do have.

It is also important to take steps towards what you hope to achieve when your request is granted. God listens to all prayers and grants the ones that are from a pure heart and with good intentions, therefore this is the best way to approach prayer

Demanding, begging or cheating will not get you anywhere, God can read your mind and knows if you deserve or not, so always pray from a pure heart and with integrity and start to make plans having faith that your prayer will be answered. This will also help your desires to manifest. Prayers that are for the highest good of all get to the front of the queue, so think about the bigger picture when you pray.

As mentioned previously, I am not a religious person but I do pray morning and night, giving thanks for the blessings in my life, usually when I am in bed. It is important to pray, God does not care where you pray, so long as you do. Remember to give thanks when you pray. We all have something to say thank you for as we are all blessed in some way.

Now that you have read a few of the spiritual laws, maybe you can look at your relationship with your partner, or your family, work colleagues or friends, in a different light. The ones you don't like are teaching you the most by acting as a mirror of your negative aspects. They are your greatest teachers and you should honour their spirit for the lessons they are showing you. Change yourself and they will change with you and you will attract people more akin to your lighter self. See yourself as happy and fulfilled and you will make your life change accordingly.

Many of us search for love and then we complain about our partners. Look again; are they a reflection of you? The trick is not to try to change them, but to change yourself. As we develop, it is sometimes necessary to move on and leave some people behind. They could be people who are bad for us or even some of our dearest friends. This can be heart breaking but it is imperative that we cut ties and move on in order to fulfil our goals and dreams. The old saying that a rolling stone gathers no moss comes to mind. Try to learn not to get too attached to people or things as they are all only on loan from God and can be gone in the blink of an eye. Practising detachment leads to a state of inner peace.

"Charaivet, charaiveti", said Gautama Buddha: Keep on moving.

I have let many people go as they were not ready for change and it hurt terribly at the time but it was the best thing I ever did. The hurt does go away and I have met some of the most wonderful people on my new path, true soul mates. I am truly blessed and grateful.

40. Seed Atoms, Life and Death

Life does not spontaneously appear in the Universe. It is constructed by architectural celestial beings. Once the personality has been created, the Universal Sons known as the Life Carriers take that life to the designated planets. Theses Sons are divided into three groups: the senior life carriers, the assistant life carriers and the custodians. The life patterns and the personalities are created by God the Father and God the Son; they are then brought to their home planet by the life carriers and through them, the divine spark and living plasm are planted via the Mother Spirit. The vital spark gives life energy to the body and mind of the new being. These sparks are referred to as permanent seed atoms.

These seed atoms contain all of the required information about the new being on a mental, astral and physical level. They are placed in the womb at the point of conception by the life carriers. When we die the energetic bodies detach from the physical body, followed by the seed atoms, the mental, the astral and the physical. The consciousness of the soul awakens in the astral state and experiences that particular bardo. When the physical seed atom is released after death, the silver chord breaks and it is recoiled and gets reinstated back into the skeletal system of the deceased. The mental is connected to the pineal, the emotional the liver and the physical the heart. The seed atoms contain the blue print records and memory of everything needed to be done by the incarnating soul, with each seed atom containing their vibrational nature. Permanent seed atoms are also planted in sacred places in order to allow a portal of light to be anchored into the planet at that point.

Later, the light body is greeted by Angels and family members who are all ready and waiting for the new arrival. My deceased nephew came to visit me during a meditation only six days after he died. He told me that his father (my brother, who died 10 months earlier) and his Uncle Arthur were waiting for him when he arrived and that gave me a great sense of peace, as I knew he was happy and supported by two people he loved very much.

I have always believed in life after death from as far back as when I was at school and a girl in my class would tell me about the ghosts in her house. I just always had an inner knowing that there was something beyond what we call death and that we were surrounded by spirit but it was not something you could speak openly about in a catholic home. As a child I always had a feeling that someone was standing behind me and to this day I am not sure whether it was my grandmother or my guardian angel Jacob, either way, I knew someone was there and as a result I very rarely felt alone or afraid.

This has since led me to question what happens when we pass over. According to Dr Deepak Chopra and his comments on near death experiences, he explains that the following happens (Taken from his book "Life after Death", page 40).

1.   The physical body stops functioning, the dying person may not be aware of this but eventually knows that this has occurred.
2. The physical world vanishes. This can happen by degrees; there can be a sense of floating upwards or of looking down upon familiar places as they recede.
3. The dying person suddenly feels lighter and freed of limitation.
4. The mind and sometimes the senses continue to operate; gradually however, what is perceived becomes non-physical.
5. A presence grows which is felt to be divine; this presence can be clothed in a light or in the body of Angels or God's. It can also communicate to the dying person.
6. Personality and memory begin to fade but the sense of "I" remains.

7. This "I" has an overwhelming sense of moving on to another phase of existence.

This seven-fold awakening is not the same as going on to heaven. Researchers often call this the inner-life phase, a transition between the mental states of being alive and the mental state of realising that one has passed on. There are many specifics that change from person to person. Not all near death experiences go into the light, some patient's report travelling to various planets in space or other worlds according to their religious beliefs. Some experience a judgement scene which can be quite harsh or hellish; it can also be full of satisfaction, however.

According to the Tibetan book of Living and Dying, we move through four bardos consisting of the following.

1. Life
2. Dying and death
3. After-death
4. Rebirth.

These are the four interlinked realities of our entire existence according to Tibetan Buddhism. Buddhists believe that life and death are one whole; death being the beginning of another chapter of life, a continual cycle of evolution and growth, always in existence in one bardo or another, just living in different levels of consciousness.

When we cross from this 3D world to the spirit world we are in the field of Akasha, the etheric field of consciousness. This is real and all previous awareness of waking and dreaming are unreal. We take a quantum leap in our conscious awareness into the infinite realm of possibilities. Apparently we are taken to where we need to be according to our belief systems. Therefore if you are a Christian you will spend time in a dimension that suits those beliefs, likewise if you are a Buddhist or a Muslim, the dimension will suit your specific needs.

The next step I believe is that you work through any unfinished business or karma in your new world. When my nephew died I had a strong urge to practice a chant I had learnt to help purify his negative karma, he thanked me for doing it when we spoke. The Tibetans use this six syllable chant "Om Benza Satto Hung." This is for healing and purification regarding the deceased. I often use it during meditations to help the souls heal when I hear of a death or a natural disaster like the Tsunami. Chanting can really help the deceased acquire a better future bardo.

My nephew was buried but in most countries and religions, the body is cremated. The reason this is done is important because they view the dead persons corpse as holding their negative karma, and when they are cremated their karma is seen to be transformed and transmuted by the flames, thus leading to a better reincarnation, the dead person is purified by the flame. Personally I prefer the idea of cremation mainly for the reason that is can be easier for the family.

My family life was hectic, my four older siblings and my nephew lived with my parents, there was always something going on with eight of us living in a three-bed roomed terrace house. When I discovered that we choose most of our major experiences in our lives (our spiritual contracts) including our mother and father and so on before we incarnate; I must admit it changed my perception vastly. I can see why I chose my parents; they were both wise old souls who lived simple, quiet lives. My sisters were like chalk and cheese, completely different. My brothers were like my dad in many ways.

I was lucky, as my karma was good, but this must be a bitter pill to swallow for those who have experienced harsh, violent or abusive lives. Choosing an abusive parent to help you work through your karma must be difficult for you to accept, nevertheless that is the case and when you accept it you can let go and move on. You chose it, the good, the bad and the ugly in order to learn and grow.

Life on Earth is short and full of tests; it is a material existence. As we gain mastery of this world, having passed these tests, we move into what are known as the mansion worlds up to and through our system constellation and Local Universe. Our spiritual development continues into the Super Universe where we are prepared for eventual transit to Havona. In the Havona worlds, we will focus on intellectual, spiritual and experiential attainment where we are set tasks in order to attain higher levels of spiritual progression. The Havona worlds are training grounds occupied by perfect beings. Understanding the make up of these perfect worlds is presently beyond human comprehension but needless to say, we will enjoy our time there. We do have leisure time on these worlds, it is not all about work.

When we have passed through these worlds, it is time for our most important sleep ever as we are prepared for our transition to the paradise that awaits us. The last transition sleep graduates a Soul into the realm of the eternal; it is a transition from one state of being to another. When we awake we are guided by beings assigned to take us to Paradise. Our arrival on Paradise signifies that we have found God, we are home.

Death is only the beginning of an eternal journey and fantastic voyage of discovery.

According to the book of Urantia, God is a multi faceted being, consisting of not only God The Father, God The Son and God the Holy Spirit but many other aspects. In general when we think of God we tend to think of one Divine Being in a singular sense and that may not be the case. The book of Urantia will open your mind and consciousness and explains creation to you in its infinite and absolute levels, talking about not only this Universe, the Super Universe, the seven Super Universes, Paradise Trinity and much more.

It explains fully the different aspects of God, the hierarchy and all of the other beings in existence from Angels and Galactic Masters to Thought Controllers and Time Lords. There are many beings in charge of each sector and Universe from The Ancient of Days, the Faithful of Days to the Divine Councillors and even Beings in charge of Paradise Trinity.

The numbers of planets habited and uninhabited in all of these Universes are far beyond the human comprehension of numbers. There are billions and trillions of these planets out there, much too far away for our limited scientific technology to discover.

41. Summary

The world is changing, mankind and the whole planet are evolving into higher levels of consciousness and a purer way of being. At 11.11am on 21^t December 2012 we will see the results of these changes both globally and universally, until then no one really knows exactly what is going to happen. I believe that there will be a phenomenal change in consciousness and our individual perception (depending on our spiritual attainment) will change the hologram we call reality, allowing us to live in a state of peace and harmony, free from lower frequency energies that temporarily pollute our planet.

There are many ways to help cope with the changes taking place but none of us can avoid the process. There are many things we can do to help purify both ourselves and the planet such as asking God to bless the food and water. Blessing it yourself uses your valuable energy; asking God to bless it uses Source energy allowing you to conserve yours. Every time it rains, I ask God to put sea salt into each drop of rain on the planet so as to cleanse the atmosphere, the earth and the waterways all over the world. Try to focus your mind on the good things in life and don't give your power to the darkness by thinking about it too much, if at all. Believe it or not, most of the destruction we see in the news is all part of the cleansing process on a global level and is part of the divine plan. Sometimes we need to go backwards in order to move forwards.

It is important to heal our own shadow self by receiving some form a complementary therapy or the practise of meditation and prayer. We also need to develop as spiritual beings in order to cope with the changes.

All of these simple things have a large effect and make a big difference, so ask God to bless you, your family and all life on Earth. There is no need to push people to change; we are all waking up in accordance with divine will so it is important to be patient with our fellow man. It is difficult not to get frustrated with our friends and families when we are awake and they are still asleep, confined to the 3rd dimension: but they will catch up. God is in charge of their awakening, it is written in the contracts they agreed before they were born, so back off and let them be.

The main thing to remember is that we are moving towards a new way of life, a perfect way of living and being. The Divine Plan is manifesting and will continue to do so until permanent change has occurred and we have evolved to higher levels of consciousness. This change is not just global it is universal. I hope you enjoy the trip and may God bless us all.

Time is precious, please us it wisely.

Love and compassion will create the peace we deserve. *Love is the Ki.*

42. Bibliography

Chris Thomas & Diane Baker – Everything you always wanted to know about your body but so far nobody's been able to tell you.

Deeprak Chopra – Life after Death

Gregg Braden – The Divine Matrix

Debbie Shapiro – Healing Mind, Healing Body

Chris Thomas – Universal Soul

Sogyal Rinpoche – The Tibetan Book of Living and Dying

Diana Cooper - A Little Light on Spiritual Laws
- Discover Atlantis

Chris Morton and Ceri Louise Thomas – The Mystery of the Crystal Skulls

Rhonda Byrne – The Secret

Mike George – The 7 Aha's of Highly Enlightened Souls

Dr Wayne W. Dyer – The Power of Intention
                  – There is a Spiritual Solution to Every Problem

Jacqueline Memory Paterson – A Tree in Your Pocket

Dalai Lama – The Little Book of Wisdom

The Urantia Foundation – The Urantia Book

THE ANGEL, THE WITCH & THE WARRIOR

Packed with information on many levels, Janine Regan-Sinclair looks at the *meaning of life, Karma, science, meditation, Angels, soul retrieval, permanent seed atoms, healing, chakras, spiritual laws, tie cutting & energy clearing, life after death and much more.* In fact there is something in here for everyone from the novice to the adept, whether you are just interested in the meaning of life or whether you are a therapist or healing practitioner, it gives brief but concise explanations and exercises to help with your journey through these mortal planes and beyond. It is meant as a taster to help you find the right path for you. The information in this book is an aid to self development and spiritual attainment; it enabled her to reach the higher levels of consciousness and to become enlightened.

Janine Regan-Sinclair is a *Crystal Ki Practitioner/ Teacher* and public speaker based in Warwickshire, United Kingdom. She developed her own healing system in 2005; *Crystal Ki Healing.* She has written articles for magazines stressing the importance of self cleansing on an energetic level. *The tie cutting and space clearing exercises in this book will teach those working with energy how to clear themselves, their home and place of work and even distance clearing.* This is essential in order to be a competent practitioner.